"If you want a permanent change, look no further. When you're through playing games, read this book and get ready for a life filled with prosperity. This program works faster than you think!"

—J. Rolan, Malibu, CA, *Developer*

"A simpler approach to wealth accumulation has never been written before and probably will never be surpassed!

—L. Anatola, New York, NY, *Educator*

"Mike Duckett is more than a financial genius, he is a teacher who makes accumulating wealth fun, simple and fast!"

—M. Taylor, Chicago, IL, *Secretary*

"I bought a copy of *Breaking the Money Barriers* for each of my children. After applying these simple techniques, they are all reaching financial independence."

—R. Adams, Los Angeles, CA, *Contractor*

"The information presented in this book will guide you to financial freedom in a very short period of time."

—E. Freedman, Manchester, England, *Teacher*

"As soon as you start reading *Breaking the Money Barriers*, your life changes and so do your finances!"

—E. Sholtz, Amsterdam, Holland, *Entrepreneur*

"This Yank knows what he's talking about! I read, I applied, and I conquered my financial problems!"

—P. Almadean, Sydney, Australia, *Minister*

"I've read this book several times and I still can't put it down! It has changed my life forever! I've made more money this month than I did in six months when I was working full-time."

—A. Marks, Ft. Lauderdale, FL, *Housewife*

Published by Whitmire Publishing, P.O. Box 669426, Marietta, GA 30066-0108, (770) 663-7071

Cover design by Imagers
Printed by Transcontinental Printing
Copyright 1998 by Michael J. Duckett
First printing April 1999

ISBN 0-9668107-0-8

Printed Canada

BREAKING

THE

MONEY BARRIERS

by

Dr. Michael J. Duckett

*To my wife, Beth, and our children,
Michael, Jr., Jason and Megan.
These spirits have taught me that
true wealth is measured not by
dollars in the pocket, but by
love in the heart.*

Contents

YOU ARE NEVER GIVEN A DREAM
WITHOUT ALSO BEING GIVEN THE
POWER TO MAKE IT COME TRUE.
HOWEVER, YOU MAY HAVE TO WORK
FOR IT.

RICHARD BACH

Introduction

When I was a little boy, I allowed my thoughts to carry me away from the extreme poverty in which I lived to a place where I knew things would be better. My seven sisters and I were orphaned and left on the streets of Detroit. We were determined to stay together at any cost! The price we paid was extreme poverty for many years. We were constantly on the run, living wherever we could find a place to sleep. Although the times were hard, we made it. I went into business for myself selling candy at the age of eight, and we soon had enough money to buy a house. It was in an inner city neighborhood, but it was home. We worked hard and had little time to play. It was during those lean times that I made up my mind to do something great with my life. I decided that I would become wealthy and help others do the same. I always had a job and several businesses. Even at lunchtime during school I would sneak away and cut a customer's lawn or sweep out a basement. I learned how to make a dollar at a young age, but I didn't learn how to *manage* it for many years. I would become wealthy and then lose it.

This pattern continued until I met a man named Leo Schrot. Leo was a retired real estate attorney who had made millions in property. He took me under his wing and taught me the essence of money. I learned everything Mr. Schrot could teach me, and then I found it was time to learn more on my own. At age sixteen, after reading Napoleon Hill's *Think and Grow Rich*, I decided to interview at least one thousand self-made millionaires. I essentially posed the same questions to each of the millionaires, and began to find some similarities. I continued this interview process for many years, and later formulated and correlated my findings. After creating a technology from the interviews, I started using this process in my own life and soon became very wealthy. I realized that if I could become wealthy with this system, I could teach others to do the same. As I shared this treasured information with friends and associates, I discovered something interesting. Each time someone used the information from my system, their life would change dramatically for the better! And they also became wealthy in a very short period of time. After owning over 180 business, I retired in my early thirties. I became bored with "feeding the pigeons," and one morning I woke up excited, remembering a dream about a greater purpose for my life. I had envisioned creating 50,000 millionaires with my technology, yet I had no idea how this would become a reality. As I started to teach others about money, how to change their belief systems and become empowered, they became wealthy. After reaching their financial dreams, they wanted to get on board and help create more millionaires with me.

At the writing of this book, we are at 9,000 millionaires and still growing! My goal is now to create 1,000,000 millionaires by helping each person create the finances necessary to live his or her life purpose. As people become wealthy and prosperous, their world improves. As one person's world improves, the entire world becomes a better place. I challenge you to study this book as if your life depended on it. Every piece of information is of value to you to help you create your dreams. This could be your last chance to make a significant change in your life. Why not seize this opportunity and savor the wealth in the following pages? As you apply this technology to your life and you experience success, please write to me. Let me know how you are doing. I love people, and I would enjoy hearing from you.

Prosperously yours,
Mike Duckett
May 12, 1998

CHAPTER 1

WHERE IT ALL

BEGAN

ALL LIMITS ARE SELF-IMPOSED.

ICARUS

The waves crashing against the side of the ship sounded like canons exploding in battle! At any moment the Niña, the Pinta and the Santa Maria could be ripped apart in the violent waters of the Atlantic. That night, like so many others on that daring voyage, was embraced with uncertainty.

As the morning sun crested the sea's horizon, the mate in the crow's nest observed a speck of something in the far distance. Restraining himself and steadying his telescope, he double-checked his vision. After several repetitions he was certain of himself, and excitedly called out to the ship's captain, "Land Ho! Land Ho!" As Christopher Columbus frantically scurried up to the viewing point, he grabbed the telescope and breathlessly observed her beauty for the first time.

Our story begins with the discovery of the Americas— land of dreams and prosperity. Although the soil was rich with nutrients, there was some uncertainty about the new land. There was also unlimited potential for those who had so recently discovered it. The original inhabitants, who came to be known as Indians, had very little commerce established. There were no towns, cities, industries, schools, markets or government. The absence of all of these and more created one important thing—a dream. The dream of making this new land a home. This dream created a need which turned into a challenge, and the challenge birthed opportunity. Opportunity is what can make a person or a nation successful and wealthy.

The opportunity this new land presented had been seen before in other places and by other people all over the globe. For millennia, people had discovered remote lands which they then developed. Tundra was turned into cities, deserts into oases, and jungles into financial centers. Although the land called America seemed to be nothing special in the beginning, its uniqueness would evolve within a hundred years after its discovery.

By the year 1610, the first settlers began their journey toward the new America and established Jamestown. Its people were average. They were hard-working, but nothing out of the ordinary. The first years in the new land proved to be difficult, and the necessary staples of goods and food were scarce. The majority of early settlers realized they had to rely on certain individuals within the settlements and indigenous communities to meet their basic needs. These individuals acquired more than the others and started to trade among themselves. This was the first sign of differences within the group of the new settlers.

Most of the settlers had come to the new world with about the same amount of wealth and worldly posses-sions. However, some looked at the opportunity in the new land differently than others. These unique few knew that if they were willing to work a little harder than the others, and create a plan for their business, then they would prosper. This was the beginning of com-merce in America.

This opportunity continues today. Of course, all oppor-tunity requires personal growth and the settling of early America was no different. The nation grew as its people responded to the challenges they faced within them-selves. This great nation continues to grow today as a result of the growth within its people.

Millionaires are created in the United States everyday. Even the poor in the United States could be considered wealthy by the standards of other countries in the world. The average "poor" American family has a stove, refrigerator, at least one television, at least one telephone, and multiple pieces of clothing. Decent schools, health care and, most important, the opportunity to earn a steady income are also available.

There are many reasons for this high standard of living even among our poor, but the number one reason is attitude. If you tell someone who lives below poverty level that you are going to take their telephone away, you would have a fight on your hands. The reason is attitude—they *expect* to have a telephone in their lives. The same goes for all the luxuries just mentioned. Inventory your own life. You have what you have because you expect it out of life and demand it of yourself.

There is an old saying that the only difference between the wealthy and the poor is *attitude*. The wealthy demand more of themselves, and are willing to take the necessary action steps to get the things they expect. In other words, opportunity is directly connected to the demands we put on ourselves. You must expect and demand more of yourself in order to get more! It is not enough to just *want* more. When you start demanding more, you will get it! The more we demand, the more opportunities we get.

It has been said that every opportunity is disguised as a problem. See the problems in your life for what they are—custom designed opportunities for growth! Your current situation is not necessarily your destiny. It is a passing opportunity that can move you toward bigger and better things. It is imperative that you *evaluate* your life along the way. The great philosopher Plato said, "An unexamined life is not worth living." Are you going where you want to go? Are you becoming the kind of person you want to become? Take a moment right now to answer these questions. If you find yourself missing your mark, or not going in the direction you want to take, make a change. To change is simple. Make the decision, and stick to your commitment for something better.

Jack is a construction worker who builds high rise buildings. Everyday at lunch all of the workers gather on the job site to eat together. Almost every day Jack opens his lunch box and yells out, "Peanut butter and jelly sandwiches. I hate peanut butter and jelly sandwiches." Finally one of the workers spoke up and said, "Jack if you don't like peanut butter and jelly sandwiches, why don't you just tell your wife to stop making them?" Jack replied, "Tell my wife? I make my own lunch!"

Many of us are making the same life for ourselves every day. We complain about how things are, yet do nothing to change. If you don't like the sandwich of life you are making everyday, use the information in this book to change your menu. It has worked extremely well for over 9,000 people, and it can work for you too!

Chapter 1 Review
Where It All Began

1.   Attitude determines what you get out of life.

2.   You must demand more out of yourself and life to become successful.

3.   Your current situation is an opportunity for more accomplishments.

4.   On a regular basis evaluate where you are, and where you are going. Ask yourself this important question, "Am I taking the action necessary to achieve my ultimate life?"

CHAPTER 2

MONEY

Riches are not an end in life,
but an instrument of life.

HENRY WARD BEECHER

M oney is such a passionate topic. So many people would love to have it, but few are willing to learn how to create it. You must learn the basics of money before you can handle it. Why?

Here's an interesting fact: If you distribute one million dollars to each person in the United States and then check back in five years, you would make an amazing discovery. The social classes would have remained exactly the same. In addition, those who were considered poor before receiving the million might even be in worse condition. They might even have bigger drug addictions, more spousal and child abuse, or bigger spending problems than before.

Money doesn't solve personal problems—it magnifies them! You must work on yourself to be able to handle money. Someone once said that the most sensitive nerve in the human body is the one that leads to the wallet. If you are a bully without money, you will become a bigger bully with money. Without self-improvement, money literally becomes a burden. With self-improvement, money is a great addition to life.

In 1924, an important meeting was held in Chicago, Illinois. Attending this meeting were some of the world's most successful financiers. This high-powered group of people were men who knew the secret of making money. There was no doubt where their main focus was. Twenty-five years after that meeting, all of these successful men had met their demise. The president of the largest independent steel company, Charles Schwab, died bankrupt after living for five years on borrowed money. The president of the greatest utility company, Samuel Insull, had been indicted on charges of fraud and embezzlement. He fled to Europe, and later came back to the U.S. He was later acquitted of the charges. The president of the largest gas company, Howard Hopson, was insane. The greatest wheat speculator, Arthur Cuttor, died abroad, insolvent. The president of the New York Stock Exchange, Richard Whitney, had just been released from Sing Sing. All of these men knew how to make money, but not one of them learned how to live. If wealth is one of your goals in life, make certain that personal development is another.

What exactly *is* money? Have you ever really thought about it? Believe it or not, money *isn't real*. It started as a concept—just like everything else we see in this world. Since a concept is simply a thought, money is nothing more than mental energy. That's right, money is simply energy. To attract more of it into your life, you must create a positive belief toward it.

Today the energy of money is represented by metal and paper, which consists of the same atoms that make up everything on this planet, including human beings. I love people! I love money! Same thing! You must love it too! Many good works can be accomplished with money. In fact, many good works can *only* be accomplished with money, especially if they are large scale.

So, money is really nothing more than an idea—an idea *backed by confidence*. The earliest commerce was based on bartering. A person might trade one pig for fifty chickens, or fifty chickens for six months of labor. This barter system was cumbersome. The governments of the time improved the system by using metal coins to represent value. What made the coins powerful? The coins were made of silver, and later gold. Since these metals were considered precious and valuable, people had *confidence* that they could trade their goods and services for the coins. This was the beginning of money, as we now know it. After the invention of paper, many governments started printing paper money in various denominations with pictures of rulers. Most people had confidence in their rulers and governments, which gave them confidence that these pieces of paper would be worth something.

If someone showed you a real $100 dollar bill, and a photocopy of a $100 bill, which would you rather have? Everyone (including children) would say the *real* one. Even though both bills look the same, you would want the *real* $100 dollar bill. You have confidence that the genuine bill could be exchanged for something of value, while the copy could not. Simply put then, money is merely a thought or idea in which we place our confidence, that it (the money) represents a certain value. This "value" is then exchanged for goods or services.

If money is given away (as in welfare) in exchange for little or no effort on the part of the recipient, it again loses its value and begins to buy less because it no longer represents the production and exchange of goods and services. This is basic economics, the science that studies the production, distribution, and consumption of goods and services.

The giving and receiving a gift or a tithe is different. Ideally, they're given out of the abundance of the heart of the giver. Ideally, the receiver accepts this gift or tithe with the understanding that she must have already given something of value to the giver or she would not be receiving a gift or tithe.

Money is a substitute for things (including information). If there is no production of things (goods and services), then there's no money! Behind any individual who needs money is the problem of low production. In order to make more money, you must produce a valuable product or service. This will add up to surplus cash. As soon as you stop producing the product or service, the exchange breaks and you stop making money.

The only other ingredient necessary to accumulating money is communication. You must get the word out about your quality product or service. Even an employer must be communicated with in order to reveal your superior work as an employee. The more people you tell about your product or service, the more people will be interested in purchasing, or obtaining them.

That's it in a nutshell. If you see an underpaid worker or an insolvent business, you know they are either not producing or not communicating adequately.

There is a simple mathematical equation to explain this concept:

Production of goods or services +
Communication to others = More Money

Unfortunately, most people aren't taught this concept today. Many expect to receive money as a gift—from inheritance, the government, or another perhaps magical source. It's no wonder that so many people believe in luck. Even criminals believe they can steal their way to wealth. Yet, how many retired criminals do you know? Usually they are incarcerated, killed, or die of some unusual disease in prison. You can't run from the person you become. If you are willing to participate in this game called *money*, you will be surrounded with its wonderful energy. The game of money is the same as any other mental or spiritual path. You must start with a mindset of wanting to do good for yourself and others. It has often been said that if you are willing to help others get what they want, you can have anything you want.

Mary, at age 38, was a talented lower level manager for a Fortune 100 company. She had worked for the company for the past twenty years, but her salary still fell short of her monthly expenses. Since it was company policy to only do annual reviews, she knew not to approach her boss for a raise.

During my consultation with Mary, we determined that she could actually earn more money working for her company as an independent consultant. Mary resigned, cashed in her retirement and signed a contract with her previous employer to do consultant work on a part time basis. Mary is now working three eight-hour days and makes $24,000 *more* a year. On the other two days she's learning about investments, trading stocks, and occasionally takes on other consulting clients.

You are *never stuck* in a job or business, though you might be temporarily detained while you explore your options. Don't hesitate to call on a professional to help you discover options or hidden talents.

Chapter 2 Review
Money

1. In order to accumulate wealth, you must be willing to learn the basics of money.

2. Money does not solve personal problems, it magnifies them. You must be willing to work on yourself.

3. Money isn't real. It's merely a thought—an idea backed by confidence.

4. Money given in the form of welfare loses its value.

5. A lack of money means inadequate production or communication of the individual or business.

CHAPTER 3

THE
BASIC TRUTHS
OF MONEY

NO ONE SHOULD BE RICH EXCEPT
THOSE WHO UNDERSTAND IT.

JOHANN WOLFGANG VON GOETHE

Being a biochemist and former research scientist, I can tell you that an idea is simply chemicals mixing in the brain. In other words—money is nothing more than an idea producing a chemical mixture in the brain. Therefore, what we think about money is what we actually experience in our lives.

It's amazing to hear thousands of intelligent people say, "I don't need to be rich, I just need enough to get by." My response is always the same—why limit yourself? Why not go for millions and then give it away! But, don't compromise and settle for less. Rita Davenport said, "Money isn't everything, but it ranks right up there with oxygen!" I've had problems when I had money, and problems when I was broke. Believe me, problems *with* money is better!

I've discovered there are a few basic truths about wealth accumulation. Look at each of these truths. Realize they are the keys to making you wealthy. The basic truths of wealth accumulation are as follows:

1.   *The inflow of money into your life must be greater than your bills.*

Although this might seem basic, most people don't realize the importance of this statement. The only way to accumulate wealth is to have more money coming in than going out. Samuel Johnson said, "Whatever you have, spend less." Wealthy people live on 30%-50% of their income and invest the balance. In other words wealthy people invest 50%-70% of their income. That is one of the ways they become so wealthy!

The average person lives on most of their income and intends to save what is left over. Unfortunately, most of the time there isn't anything left to save! Usually, people adjust their spending to the amount of money they earn. Whether you make $100 a week or $100,000, you won't keep any of your money unless you understand and apply the principles of wealth accumulation and investing.

When more money comes into your life, invest it. Maintain your current lifestyle as if nothing had changed. If you aren't making ends meet, consider producing more income and reducing your current lifestyle. Though this may be difficult at first, try it on a temporary basis until you achieve your financial independence.

2.   *You must exchange your product, service or time for more than it costs you.*

No matter what your business is, the objective is to make a profit. By making a profit, you will be able to expand your business and purpose. Even churches need to make a profit or there will be no place for their congregation to meet. Even Mother Theresa, the great humanitarian, had to make a profit in order to stay in the business of helping the needy!

Don't be afraid to ask for money in exchange for your product, service, or time. If you can't get over this block on your path to success ask yourself, "Why am I trying to keep wealth away from myself?" If you don't feel worthy of asking for money you will either have to get over it, or learn to enjoy being broke!

Why not become wealthy and then share your wealth with charities, your church, the poor, and so on? You can do much more for other people if you are willing to become wealthy just by asking for your fair share. You will also feel better about yourself and radiate confidence to others. *You are worth it!*

We usually have difficulty respecting people who have money hang-ups. The subconscious mind picks up the lack of self-confidence in the person who is insecure about money. If this person lacks respect for himself, how are we supposed to have it for him?

After twelve years of chiropractic practice, Dr. Johnson was ready to call it quits. He said he felt burned out and was no longer excited about adjusting his patients. During our consultation, Dr. Johnson discovered that he wasn't really tired of his profession, but was discouraged in his attempts to collect money from his patients and insurance companies. Dr. Johnson was so reluctant to collect money that some of his more wealthy patients had actually been receiving free chiropractic care for over two years!

The root of Dr. Johnson's financial problems were not in the running of his office. The doctor had some childhood memories of never being taken to the doctor's office when ill because his parents felt that a doctor's visit was a waste of money. After Dr. Johnson cleared up this issue in his mind, he made an additional $150,000 that year.

3. *Money is simply a reflection of your productivity.*

The more you produce, the more money you will have in your life. This is especially true if you are producing something that relates to your life's purpose. What should you produce? Whatever you love, or what your livelihood is at this time.

I was once hired by a real estate broker who wanted to increase her business. When I walked into the office for our meeting, my client and a few of her sales people were sitting around laughing and joking. Although there isn't anything wrong with having a good time at work, there is a problem if it gets in the way of production.

After we determined what would bring more money into the business, the sales people were taught action steps to increase productivity, which resulted in additional income to everyone in the business. Once the employees realized that their individual incomes were directly related to their personal productivity, and took the necessary action, money flowed immediately into that business.

4.   *Your personal happiness is directly related to the quantity and quality of exchange in your life.*

The more you are exchanging with others, the more you will experience happiness in your life. If you are feeling depressed, force yourself into a giving state and you will lift yourself back into happiness. Although this may sound like a "pollyanna" philosophy, it is simply a fact of life. We are truly happy when we are producing, especially if we are doing it for others.

5.   *Money magnifies your personal problems.*

Ralph was the kind of guy that people loved to be around, until Ralph had a few drinks. With a wife, three children and a full time job, Ralph limited his drinking to the weekends. When the weekend rolled around, Ralph had a few beers and gave his family (and anyone else that was nearby) a hard time.

One Friday, Ralph took the day off from work, and drove from Atlanta to Florida, in order to purchase one of the first lottery tickets. Ralph won $22 million! His life was changed forever! He was to receive over one million dollars a year for twenty years! Ralph immediately called his preacher and told him to put the addition on the church that would cost $370,000. On Ralph's commitment, the preacher hired a local contractor and completed the beautiful addition to their church. Two years later, the church had to sue Ralph in bankruptcy court for the $370,000. For a person who was receiving over a million dollars a year, how did Ralph go broke? Quite simply, Ralph had not developed the mindset to handle the extra money.

An IRS study showed that almost 80% of all lottery winners are broke within five years of receiving their initial winnings. Many times people who inherit or win large sums of money will lose it rapidly. They do not have the consciousness necessary to keep money in their lives.

6.   *Welfare degrades money and the person receiving it because there's no exchange.*

When a person receives something without giving something, they are not in a proper state of exchange. The result of being "out of exchange" is that the person on the receiving end does not respect or value the item they have received. For example, when people are given money in the form of government services, they begin to feel enslaved since they did not contribute to earning that money. One of the biggest reasons is that they do not appreciate the amount of welfare, meager as it is, and they begin to look at money as worthless. You must be willing to "exchange" in your life to keep money flowing around you.

Everything you see in the world was at one time merely a thought in someone's mind. Everyone has the internal power to turn a thought or idea into a physical object. If you wish to bring a thought into the material world, you must make a plan, set some goals and take consistent action on those goals.

Imagine yourself taking a deep breath and swimming under water for twenty or thirty feet. You think to yourself, "No problem. This is nice." You would probably enjoy it. Now imagine that as you took that deep breath and dove under the surface, your suit snagged on something. At first, you would focus on getting yourself untangled because you know that in a minute or so you would be running out of air. At this time, you just "want" air and there is no urgency, probably only a sense of annoyance.

But, after that minute is up, your effort to free yourself would become much more intense! Before much longer you would be ripping a gaping hole in your suit if that's what it took to set yourself free! Your panic is generated by your *need* for air.

At first you merely wanted to be set free. Then that feeling changed to a need. That need or *determination* is exactly what it takes to develop the mental self-discipline necessary to become truly successful on your quest to financial freedom. You must ask yourself, "Have I had enough of living in my present circumstances to make some definite changes?" Then, ask yourself, "Do I merely *want* these changes, or am I *DETERMINED?*"

You must create your desire as a need. Everyone "wants" money and wealth, but only about 2% of the public feel that they "need" it. They are the ones who

34

have it! To acquire wealth, simply adopt the successful habits of people who have large amounts of money. As you do this, you will begin to see money flow into your life. One of the main thoughts a wealthy person has about money is that they want to be in "exchange." This word must be totally understood before you can attempt to be responsible enough to acquire large amounts of wealth.

One major problem that most humans have is a natural propensity to be negative. It often seems that it is much easier to focus on the negative, complain about something, or talk about all your problems. Most people haven't learned how to control their negative thought impulses in order to create a better life for themselves. Anyone can be average! According to the IRS, the average American is broke. Perhaps you are reading this book because you have reached the point of passionately wanting a better life for yourself. If so, you are now ready to develop positive mental discipline.

Do you merely want wealth, or do you *need* wealth? There is a major difference. And the effects of the want or need will be a determining factor in your wealth accumulation.

Chapter 3 Review
The Basic Truths Of Money

The basic truths of wealth accumulation are as follows:

1. The inflow of money into your life must be greater than your spending.

2. You must exchange your product, service or time for more than it costs you.

3. Money is simply a reflection of your productivity.

4. Your personal happiness is directly related to the quantity and quality of exchange in your life.

5. Money magnifies your personal problems.

6. Welfare systems degrade money and the person receiving it because there is no exchange.

CHAPTER 4

EXCHANGE

THE UNIVERSE OPERATES
THROUGH DYNAMIC EXCHANGE.

LIKE A RIVER, MONEY MUST
KEEP FLOWING, OTHERWISE IT
BEGINS TO STAGNATE, TO
CLOG, TO SUFFOCATE AND
STRANGLE ITS VERY OWN LIFE
FORCE. CIRCULATION KEEPS IT
ALIVE AND VITAL

DEEPAK CHOPRA

When we talk about money we must understand the concept of *exchange*, which is a basic economic term. What does it mean and how does it affect personal prosperity? Exchange refers to the cycle of giving and receiving something of value. Receiving is incomplete without giving, and vice versa. This is the key to prosperity in general, not just with money.

In order to be involved in exchange to increase your wealth, you must be willing to create a valuable product or service. Your valuable product or service must then be exchanged for something else of value. You can't give your product or services away for free, nor can you expect others to do the same. Money represents a given value for the goods or services that are exchanged. Benjamin Franklin said, "If you can't pay for a thing, don't buy it. If you can't get paid for it, don't sell it. Do this and you will have calm and drowsy nights, with all of the good business you have now and none of the bad."

Many people have a problem with the idea of exchanging something valuable for something of value. One thing is certain: no wealthy person would have that problem. If you disagree, it is because you're not thinking like the wealthy.

Because money is nothing more than thought energy, thoughts opposing wealth create poverty, while thoughts receptive to wealth create wealth. It really is as basic and simple as that.

Surprisingly, most of our thoughts about money and prosperity are not ours. These thoughts have been passed down to us through generations. If most of the ancestors before you were impoverished or barely getting by, then you can be sure that your beliefs about money are going to be based around poverty.

If you come from a background of lack in any form, you must break that pattern. Changing this pattern isn't as hard as it might seem, since it starts with a simple decision.

Sherry was extremely worried about getting robbed and losing all of her money. When I asked her about the origin of this fear, we found out that her grandparents had been robbed in New York when they first arrived in America. Although they had brought suitcases full of money, the thieves took everything leaving her grandparents penniless and on the street. Sherry had heard this story since childhood and subconsciously believed that this could happen to her. I reassured her that if her grandparents had taken adequate precautions to protect their money, it would not have been stolen.

Sherry realized the origin of her fear and *decided* not to be preoccupied with the idea of being robbed. Then she immediately took steps to properly protect her money. When the fear started to slip back into her thinking, she would gently remind herself that she had already made the decision to change and had taken the actions necessary to deal with the fear.

Chapter 4 Review
Exchange

1. The term *exchange* refers to the cycle of giving something valuable in exchange for receiving something valuable.

2. Our beliefs around money are not ours, these thoughts have been passed down for many generations.

3. Beliefs opposing wealth can be changed by deciding to do so, and following up the decision with appropriate action.

CHAPTER 5

DECISION

ONE DAY, ALICE CAME TO A FORK
IN THE ROAD AND SAW A CHESHIRE
CAT IN A TREE. 'WHICH ROAD DO I
TAKE?' SHE ASKED, 'WHERE DO YOU
WANT TO GO?' WAS HIS RESPONSE.
'I DON'T KNOW,' ALICE ANSWERED.
'THEN,' SAID THE CAT, 'IT DOESN'T
MATTER.'

LEWIS CARROLL

THE ROADS WE TAKE ARE MORE
IMPORTANT THAN THE GOALS WE
ANNOUNCE.
DECISIONS DETERMINE DESTINY.

FREDERICK SPEAKMAN

I sn't it amazing how our thoughts are constantly creating something for us? Good or bad outcomes begin with the collective thoughts we generate moment to moment. What you experience in life is the result of your predominant thoughts.

Decision is the most powerful of all thoughts because it is the force behind change. It is also one of the most abused and neglected of all thought forms. Many people think they are making a decision about something when they are actually doing nothing more than entertaining themselves. When you decide to do something (or not do something), the result is a specific change involving action around that habit or situation. The problem is that most people say, "I would like to lose weight," or, "I would like to stop smoking," but in reality they are doing nothing more than wishing it were so. They don't intend to actually stop their negative habit. Since they're not sincere about changing their habits, they're setting themselves up for failure. They are actually sabotaging themselves.

Isn't it strange that we can be so cruel to ourselves when we would be fighting mad if someone else tried to do that to us? The difference between making a clear decision and just wishing it were so is the degree of commitment to ourselves. Don't play games with yourself! Decide to do something and then follow through with it, or don't "decide" at all.

If you are truly making a decision, then you are firmly determining the outcome of that decision. If you don't want to make a decision around your life, don't play games with your mind. Simply skip the decision and keep eating, smoking or whatever. Only when you are committed to yourself with *determination* should you make a decision. A decision made with determination shifts you into a different belief system, as well as action. If you are willing to shift into a different belief system, your problem will be short lived.

Let's look at how we could shift into a different belief system about weight loss, then we will use it to change our wealth. If you have a weight problem and have been dieting for years with no results, all you have to do is make a decision to change your beliefs around food. First, understand that food is a necessity, not a pleasure. If you change this belief you will eat to survive and not gorge yourself for fun. If you begin to think of yourself as a "health nut" and do the things healthy people do, you will lose weight. If you are not sure that you want to commit to that drastic of a change, okay. But you must realize that you are not going to lose weight, or lose weight permanently if there is no commitment.

The same principle of decision pertains to the accumulation of wealth. You must decide that you are going to become wealthy and then proceed with the necessary steps to make it happen in your life. First, decide how much money you want and what type of lifestyle would make you comfortable. Next, locate people who are making the kind of money and living the lifestyle that you want, and talk to them. Tell them your intentions of becoming wealthy and ask for their suggestions. Take notes! This information is far too valuable to leave to memory. After interviewing at least a half dozen or more wealthy people, look at your notes and decide what you need to learn. Then go into action!

There are people who think they are above money. They are not wealthy. They may even be disguised as poor clergy or a spiritual person. It may be their belief that they should only concentrate on things of a spiritual nature. They forget they are still in the physical world. In this physical realm, you not only need money to survive, it will also help your spiritual mission. God never asked us to be poor. Instead, God wants prosperity to be our gift from him.

Wealth has been achieved by people of all classes, intellect and nature. Money is not beyond anyone's reach, but it could be beyond their beliefs. Start now by telling yourself with conviction, "If others can do it, so can I."

Chapter 5 Review
Decision

1. Our predominant thoughts (good or bad) are constantly creating our lives.

2. Decision is the most powerful of all thought forms because it has the power to create positive change.

3. You must decide to become wealthy and then be willing to put forth the necessary work.

4. Everyone needs money to live.

5. Everyone is capable of producing a fortune if they are willing to put forth the effort.

CHAPTER 6

EDUCATION

EDUCATION IS NOT MERELY A
MEANS OF EARNING A LIVING OR
AN INSTRUMENT OF ACQUISITION
OF WEALTH. IT IS AN INITIATION
INTO LIFE OF SPIRIT, A TRAINING
OF THE HUMAN SOUL IN THE
PURSUIT OF TRUTH AND THE
PRACTICE OF VIRTUE.

VIJAYA LAKSHMI PANDIT

*

WHAT YOU GET BY
ACHIEVING YOUR GOALS IS
NOT AS IMPORTANT AS
WHAT YOU BECOME BY
ACHIEVING THEM.

ZIG ZIGLAR

Y ou might be lacking knowledge about the subject of money ranging from the stock market and real estate to computers, taxes and so on. Make a plan for your course of study. You can pursue study gradually, which will result in a gradual accumulation of wealth. Or you can jump into your study with the enthusiasm of a sprinter in the 100-yard dash. Of course, the sprinter will get to his destination at a faster rate. You decide your pace, but remember to stick to your decision.

The first place you should visit is the public library. Get books on the subjects that you have decided will be necessary to achieve your wealth. Learning is one of the most critical aspects to accumulating wealth, second only to decision.

Due to a very impoverished childhood and little education, I decided at a young age to better my life financially. I worked for money, but did not apply myself in school. I found myself to be an "existing idiot." I would rise to a certain level of wealth and then fall back down. I finally realized that I would have to start studying if I planned to stay wealthy.

I studied on my own, and after two years in the U.S. Army, applied to college. I was unable to pass the entrance exam. I continued to study my weakest subjects and soon was admitted to a local college. Since I had no educational foundation, I had to study hard. For years, most of my waking hours were devoted to studying. I pushed on because I knew that I needed more information about how to handle money, my business and my life.

I received my two-year degree, then a four-year degree, and finally my first doctorates. I decided to go on for more. After my degrees in the sciences, I decided to get additional education in business, and ultimately law.

Currently, I am working toward my master's degree in Theology. I don't know if I will ever stop learning because it makes the world more understandable. The more we understand, the less scary any subject becomes. With less fear there is more enjoyment in life.

Although formal education is fun, it is not a necessity. That's right, formal education is good for some things, but it is not a necessity for the accumulation of money. You are probably thinking that it is easy for me to say, since I have many degrees. However, the main purpose of a formal education is to teach us the discipline of learning. Most people who reach a degreed status at a university will continue to learn on their own for the rest of their lives.

Formal education does give us one other benefit—a structured, accelerated learning format. It might be difficult to be motivated to read three or four hundred-page books in three or four months. When you are enrolled in a college course, you might find yourself doing just that multiple times in one semester because your instructors require it. The requirement will motivate you to get through the material at an accelerated rate, with understanding. Although college can be a fun place, it is not a necessary requirement for the accumulation of money.

If you are willing to study business, finance or taxes thirty to sixty minutes every day, you will become an expert on any of these subjects within two or three years. To be an expert does not mean you know everything about a subject. An expert only knows twenty percent of any subject well, but has the ability to locate information on the other eighty percent. It takes a little discipline to commit yourself to study daily, so if you don't have it, you might have to enroll in a local college or university.

It is easy to learn and it is also easy not to learn. The same is true of wealth. It is easy to become wealthy, and it is easy not to become wealthy. If you want to learn or earn, you must decide you will do it and then stick with it for the rest of your life. All wealthy people are eager to learn and earn. You would be amazed to find out how many wealthy people never finished high school. That does not mean they are not interested in learning. They would not have their wealth if they were not willing to learn on a daily basis.

If you do not have the necessary knowledge to manage your money, then you will lose it. There is nothing more painful in life than to make millions, and then lose it all as a result of incompetence.

There is a term used in the computer industry called "chunking." It refers to taking a large project and breaking it down into a number of smaller jobs. By chunking a project, we can accomplish an amazing amount of work over a relatively short period of time. If you read four pages a day (chunking) on business or finance, you will read almost 1500 pages a year. If you are reading four pages with the intention of gaining knowledge, in four years you will have acquired ap-proximately 6000 pages of critical knowledge on money. You will be able to converse with just about anyone and be on a mental level equal to the most successful investors.

The most important change in your finances will occur as a result of this new knowledge. You will experience a different consciousness around money. It will not be a foreign subject to you anymore. Remember, if you are familiar with a topic, your fears are lessened or perhaps even eliminated. With your fears gone, you will be willing to play with this energy called money.

Chuck was a computer software sales representative for a large corporation. He had been employed with this company for over twenty years and had previous sales experience. When we started working together, Chuck made the comment that he was not interested in investments, stocks, taxes, or any of those other subjects dealing with money. I told him that if he wanted more money, he had to develop a desire to learn about the subjects dealing with money.

Chuck began by reading the *Wall Street Journal* a few times a week and two pages daily from a book on stock investing. A few weeks later, he was reading more pages from the stock investing book and had subscribed to the *Wall Street Journal*.

Within six months, Chuck had received a substantial raise, and was investing in the stock market. He had also developed a voracious appetite for knowledge on the subject of money. Incidentally, Chuck's annual income doubled within nine months.

Knowledge is power! When you acquire knowledge around the subjects concerning money, you develop power around it. Power helps us manage and acquire more of this stuff called money!

Chapter 6 Review
Education

1. Make a plan of action to acquire the necessary knowledge to make more money.

2. Formal education is a good discipline but not necessary to accumulating wealth.

3. If you study as little as thirty minutes per day, you can become an expert on any subject within two years.

4. Chunking is a powerful way to learn any subject in a relatively short period of time.

5. Increasing your knowledge about money increases your power over it, bringing even greater wealth.

CHAPTER 7

BELIEFS

WE ARE WHAT WE THINK.
ALL THAT WE ARE ARISES
FROM OUR THOUGHTS.
WITH OUR THOUGHTS, WE
MAKE OUR WORLD.

THE BUDDHA

UNDER ALL THAT WE THINK,
LIVES ALL WE BELIEVE, LIKE
THE ULTIMATE VEIL OF OUR
SPIRITS.

ANTONIO MACHADO

B eliefs are the filters through which we accumulate money. Depending on what we believe, money will be attracted either toward or away from our lives. It is important that you realize how beliefs affect your wealth and life.

If you want to make things better for yourself, then you must change internally, starting with your beliefs. I am amazed when people tell me they want to create a different financial scenario for themselves, but they are not willing to apply the discipline necessary to change unwise beliefs.

Your life is a system of behaviors based on your beliefs and habits. Your financial success is a by-product of that system. If money is not flowing into your life, it's because your system is not working. If you continue to repeat the lifestyle habits you have learned up until now, you will get more of the same lifestyle tomorrow. Even if you have tried and failed many times, you can still change your life by changing your beliefs. The truth is that rich people think differently than the average person. They have different beliefs and expectations about money, and therefore, they experience a different reality or lifestyle.

Acquiring wealth is as simple as the decision to acquire it. Wealthy people began their search for wealth by deciding to passionately live their life's purpose, to serve others and to accept wealth along the way.

Everyone creates their own reality. Wealthy people are no exception. My reality as a child was utter poverty. My seven sisters and I lived on the streets of Detroit. We were malnourished, abused and neglected. I share this with you not to generate sympathy, but to tell you that I knew I had to create a different reality if my sisters and I were going to change our circumstances. As I grew up, I had to continually reevaluate my goals and my beliefs about money because I was changing from a poverty mindset to one of prosperity. For example, in my early years I believed that there was never enough money, and that it was out of my reach.

Finally, a wealthy friend told me that if I wanted to become wealthy, I would have to change my beliefs about money. He said I could create whatever I imagined just by working on my goals consistently. All of us have this same opportunity.

Ask yourself this question, "What are my beliefs about money?" Stop right now for just a moment and write a couple of paragraphs to answer this important question. The assumptions about money that you grew up with are crucial. You arrived at those assumptions based on your own experience and that of your ancestors, and your observations of those around you. These beliefs and assumptions became your reality. Your reality acts as a filter between you and the world.

An experiment was conducted that explains how this filter works. Researchers took a large fish and put it in an aquarium with hundreds of minnows. The fish ate the minnows. Then the researchers separated the fish from the minnows with a piece of glass. It soon realized that no matter how hard it tried, the minnows were out of reach. Finally, the researchers lifted the glass and once again allowed the minnows to swim freely all around the fish. But, it had been programmed to believe that the minnows were out of its reach forever. The poor fish literally starved to death in the presence of his favorite meal!

This same phenomenon occurs with people and money. The average person thinks, "What is the use in attempting to become wealthy? It is impossible for me." Watch out for those ancestral beliefs! Your rigidly held assumptions can be fatal to your well-being. If you believe that wealth is out of your reach, then it is. It's simply a decision. Decide you are wealthy. Make wealth your mindset and you will become wealthy.

Two renowned psychiatrists, Eric Berne and Sigmund Freud taught that each of us has a parent-ego state that remains with us psychologically. We never totally rid ourselves of our father and mother. We can actually go beyond that. Your father had parents and your mother had parents. Your grandparents had parents, and so on. As I stated earlier, they are all reflected in your beliefs. The good news is that there is a way to change these learned patterns. As you change your beliefs, you will change these learned patterns for yourself as well as for future generations!

When you realize your old beliefs about money are no longer working for you, a decision to change them must be made. If you want to become wealthy, your beliefs about money need to match the money beliefs of the wealthy. Here are several common beliefs the wealthy have about money:

1.   *Attitude is everything.*

There are no money problems, only attitude problems. Develop the right attitude and the money will follow. Your attitude has to be one of valuing wealth if it is your desire to acquire large sums of money. You must think like a wealthy person. You must not worry about not having enough money. Instead, concentrate on how you can provide a better service or product for others.

If you find yourself facing a situation (never a problem) with money, simply think, plan, and take action to resolve the challenge. Wealthy people are never beaten. They keep going until they get what they want. We all face challenges, but the wealthy never let these challenges control their destiny. Money challenges will always be around you. If you are going to play the game of big money, you need to accept the responsibility of not concentrating on the problem. Instead, put all of your effort on finding solutions, and then acting on those solutions.

Today, your are able to handle a number of large problems that you were not able to cope with ten years ago. This is because you have grown to a new level of understanding. The same growth will occur with your accumulation of wealth. You will grow to new levels of responsibility and understanding and in turn, your wealth grows too.

2. *You must face your fears.*

Anyone lacking money must have a fear of money. Fear is the only thing that can keep money out of a person's life. This fear causes the average person to want to spend their money because they are afraid they do not have enough or will lose what little they have. Of course, irresponsible spending creates more of a deficit in their cash reserves, which increases the fear of losing money. The whole problem snowballs into more money problems and greater fears around it.

The fear of money is one of the greatest barriers holding people back from their true wealth. A wealthy person is not afraid of money and, in fact, wants more of it to enjoy for obvious reasons. They spend frugally because they are comfortable with having money in their lives. In this manner, the wealthy person accumulates more money.

When a wealthy person spends money, they take an extra minute of time at the checkout counter to write the check and its amount in their checkbook register, or make a note on the receipt to later categorize their expenses. The wealthy person wants to keep track of every penny spent and knows where their money is going. This is not a matter of being cheap. This behavior shows a healthy respect for money. The more you respect money, the more wealth will come into your life.

Mark and Leonard had been good friends for many years. They had worked together to build their business into a multimillion dollar company. One day Leonard went out to pick up lunch for Mark and himself. When Leonard returned, he handed Mark his lunch and change and proceeded to his office. Suddenly Mark yelled out, "Hey, where is my nickel? You shorted me a nickel!" Leonard protested saying he had kept Mark's money separate and that the girl at the restaurant must have shorted him. One of the company managers heard the argument and offered to give them both a quarter if they would just drop the subject. Mark and Leonard both looked at this manager with confusion and outrage. Mark said, "A nickel is money and that is why we have the kind of money we have. We're concerned with every penny." The manager learned an important lesson that day—every penny counts!

3. Watch the crowd, then go in the other direction.

If you're doing something the rest of the people aren't (like investing at the beginning of the month, delaying gratification, and so on), then you are on the right track to becoming wealthy. Did you know that 98% of Americans are broke? You'd better be going in the opposite direction! J. Paul Getty, one of the wealthiest men in America, if not the world, said, "I buy when other people are selling." When other people tell you that your new-found ideas about money are wrong, take it as confirmation that you are on the right path! You must decide what you want, make plans to get it, and take action on your plans. Constantly revising this cycle of goals, plans and action will give you a guaranteed route to success.

Only about 2% of our population write goals. A very small percentage of the people in the world live their lives with a plan. An even smaller percentage of the populace take action towards their goals and plans. Compared to most of the population then, being wealthy is an exception to the rule. If someone comments about how you think differently about money, thank them and know that you are on the right path.

Colleen never wrote goals because she felt that she was too busy to be bothered with such a trivial thing. As I worked with Colleen, I explained that goals would not only make things happen in her life, but would save her time. After writing goals for six months, Colleen saw that many of her goals had been achieved, and she was able to handle the demands of her day much more effectively. I find it curious that so many people say they are "too busy" to apply tools that would help them be more successful.

The most important goal writing tool is the Things To Do list. Since most people do not write down their goals it stands to reason that only a few create a Things To Do list. This little tool will give you three times the life you are currently living.

4.   All opportunities are disguised as problems.

If you are currently having a money problem, it is actually an opportunity to create more wealth in your life. Until you find answers, you need to continually ask yourself questions about your money problems. Remember that mistakes are simply opportunities for you to gain positive feedback about your life.

Everyone has problems. That's life! In order to be successful, you must look at each problem as an opportunity to learn something. Remember when you were in school and the teacher gave you homework? The problems were given to you to help you learn the subject. Our problems in life are there to help us learn our life lessons. Thomas Edison said, "Many of life's failures are people who did not realize how close they were to success when they gave up." The main thing you must realize when you're dealing with problems is this: Never quit! Successful people may fall, but they never fail. When a problem arises that knocks you to your knees, simply brush yourself off and keep going.

Brad was driving to Atlanta from Nashville to attend one of my seminars. He had scheduled his trip to make it just in time for the seminar. Halfway to Atlanta, his car started to smoke and soon quit completely. He thought, "Well, Dr. Duckett always says that every problem is an opportunity for something great to happen. I sure want to see how this is going to turn into something great!" Well, after Brad had been sitting in his disabled car for a few minutes, a pickup truck pulled over and a young man, asked, "Need some help?" Brad replied that he needed a lift to the nearest phone or service station. The young man drove him to his family's service station while his car was being towed in. Although Brad was concerned about missing the seminar, he was more worried about getting his car fixed. The mechanic determined that Brad's car needed a new fuel pump. Since it was Saturday, it would be Monday before the station could get one. He authorized them to repair the vehicle and asked for a ride to the nearest hotel. The young man said that his sister was heading out within a few minutes and would be glad to give him a ride to the next exit where the hotel was located. When Brad got into the young lady's car, she asked where he had been heading when his car broke down? Brad told her that he was going to Atlanta to a seminar. The pretty young lady started laughing. They soon discovered that they were going to the same seminar in Atlanta, and decided to drive together. The last time I heard from this young couple they were engaged to be married. Every problem carries with it a seed for equal or greater success.

5.   *Until you know the value of something, most things appear to be worthless.*

You have the ability to substantially increase your income and change your life with the information in this book. The catch is, you must put value on this information and go into action. Study this information by reading it over and over again as if your life depended on it. Your future life as a wealthy person does depend on it!

Take notes each time you read it and soon you will discover there is gold in these words. This could be your last chance to accumulate wealth. If you treat it as your last chance, you will discover a change of life and wealth beyond your wildest dreams.

6. He who lives by the Golden Rule, gets the gold here too.

Truly wealthy people are not out to take advantage of another person's weakness. They believe life, business, and finance should be a win-win situation. The golden rule simply states, "Do unto others as you would have them to do unto you." Look for ways to serve others and you will automatically find money being attracted to you.

When dealing with other people or businesses, try to see how you can help them to solve a problem or make more money. By helping others make more money, you in turn will make more money. Everyone wins when you live by the Golden Rule. Lasting power and wealth can only be maintained by treating others as you would like to be treated. This lesson of the Golden Rule is the most universal lesson taught in all religions. *Every* holy book or scripture ever written has some form of the Golden Rule. It is one of the most important lessons we can learn.

7. Money is attracted to great ideas.

We all have hidden or untapped potential if we look deep enough to find it. Inventory yourself by writing down all of your experiences and qualities. Next, ask yourself which of these experiences or qualities would other people be willing to pay you money to share with them. Look at your current employment and ask, "How can I become more valuable to my employer so I can get a raise?" Then take the appropriate action.

Look around you where you are currently sitting. Look at every item in your home or office. Everything started with an idea and someone has profited from that idea.

Since we are all from God, we all have the same ability to create. Simply try to find ways to make people happier. These ideas can be in the form of new inventions, better service or improvements on existing things. With your intention to make other people happy, you will find that an infinite number of ideas come to you. Write these ideas down, even if they do not make sense to you at the time. Keep an idea book that you can refer to and update regularly. This is a priceless tool.

Another way to create ideas is with a small brainstorming group. Form a group of two to twelve people for the purpose of brainstorming ideas. The group should agree that no idea is stupid or irrelevant, and that no criticism or ridicule is allowed during these sessions. As the group members start to share their ideas aloud, one person should be responsible for writing them down. You would be amazed to find out how many of our greatest discoveries and inventions were the product of a brainstorming session.

8. *You are your own wealth.*

All of us have an unlimited potential to create a magnificent amount of money. First, we must realize that this principle is within ourselves, and then we must be willing to cherish this valuable thought by believing in ourselves. How do you come to believe in yourself? By taking action and never giving up!

God is a creator. Since we are created in God's likeness, then we are co-creators. We can create prosperity, just like God. Some of our great philosophers and educators believe that we do not learn anything, we simply relearn (or remember) what we already know. Perhaps that is how child prodigies are able to play the piano, or do complex math problems. These individuals already know how to do their tasks, they simply didn't forget like the rest of us. For some reason in their birthing process into this world, they were able to retain this information.

Know the power that is within you and act on that greatness! Remember that having faith in your divine greatness is a compliment to God. With the Universal power in all of us, we can overcome anything in our lives. Do not waste this power, as most people do, simply by not recognizing it. Know it is there, act like it is there, and soon you will *see* it is there.

9.   *Realize that networking saves legwork.*

The fastest way to wealth is to approach it as a group. If you form a group to go into a business venture, you will achieve success in a fraction of the time. Also, a group reduces the chances of a business going under. Each person could be a major asset to helping you become wealthy. Collect names, addresses, and telephone numbers of as many people as possible. Write an initial letter to every person you meet in a business setting. Then, periodically send a form letter to your mailing list. By doing this, your new acquaintances will be updated on you and your business. This list of individuals can be a valuable source when it is time to sell your product or service in the future. A sense of trust will already have been established. They know you are a person of integrity who has their interests in mind, and will desire what you are selling if it meets their need.

According to the IRS, the average Korean family comes to America penniless. Most will reach millionaire status in five years. One of the key ingredients in their achievement of wealth is that they work together. After all, working together is what built this great country in the first place.

Another way a group can help you to achieve your goals quickly is by forming what is known as a Mastermind Group. The concept of masterminding goes back to ancient times, and is still used today by many successful people and organizations. You can form a mastermind group by getting a group of six to twelve people together. This group should meet on a weekly basis with the purpose of supporting and visualizing each other's goals. Have one rotating chairperson who will run the meeting from beginning to end. The position of chairperson should be rotated each week to ensure that everyone gets a regular chance to head the meeting, and that no one person is in charge of the group. Everyone should sit in a circle or around a table symbolizing the equality of each member. The meeting is started with a prayer. Most mastermind groups choose prayers based around knowing that the power of God is working in their lives and in their group. Then, the first person states their mastermind request to the group. Then, each group member visualizes the first person's request and states that visualization aloud. After going around the entire group, this process is repeated for each member's visualization.

It has been said that all thoughts are energy, which once created, cannot be destroyed. Thoughts continue to exist as they leave us and wander into the universe. When one person prays, the energy created is one person's energy. But, when two people pray, the energy is equal to two to the second power, or four. The number continues to grow, as we bring more and more people into the same prayer. That is powerful praying, and that is the power of a mastermind group.

10. Establish the habit of success.

Successful people study success. Read, listen to tapes, and attend seminars regularly on the subjects of success and money. By continuing your education on success, you will be exposed to new information and people which will promote your growth. If you are interested in accumulating additional money in your life, you must do what all the millionaires before you have done. You must continue to learn more about money—how to create it in your life and manage it. The only way to do this is by committing yourself to a regular study program on the subject of money. It might seem a little boring at first, but you have to create curiosity around it. Every effort no matter how small, whether it be reading every day, listening to a tape, or attending seminars, will mean a substantial monetary return later.

Another way to develop the habits of the successful is to do what successful people do, go where they go, and think like they think. Copy them in every way possible (within your budget). When I was a little boy, everyday I wore men's dress shirts and ties I bought from the Goodwill because in my mind I was living a different reality. People made fun of me, but I didn't care. I was determined to make a better life for myself and my sisters. And I did! Don't *ever* give up! The saying, "Fake it 'til you make it" is more important on your road to success than you could ever imagine.

11. Share your wealth.

Tithe to people and organizations that are in need of your support or who give you spiritual guidance. Since money is energy, you must keep finances flowing through your life—in and out. Tithing is the only way you can keep the flow of finances activated. If you stop giving, you will stop your flow. There is no way around this—give regularly.

Another name for tithing is *reciprocal maintenance*, which means that to regularly maintain what is coming to you, you must give back on a regular basis. All wealthy people know the power of reciprocal maintenance. My wife and I have a weekly meeting to discuss our finances. One of the most exciting parts of this meeting is to decide where we are going to tithe. This single action is extremely empowering. It sets the power of the entire universe into motion specifically for you. Many clients over the years have said that reciprocal maintenance is the biggest causal factor in their prosperity. When you give, do so without expecting anything in return. I always get a laugh out of people who write a check so they can get a tax write-off. That's not giving, that's an investment. If you are giving with the intention of receiving a return, even if it is to a church, forget it. You'll lose your gamble on receiving a return. If you are giving from your heart because you want to give back to God, then you will receive abundance in return.

Wealthy people understand that in actuality they don't really own anything; they are merely the custodian of all they receive from their efforts. As a custodian, giving back to God is a blessing and a source of joy. I always give cash. I don't want a receipt and I don't want anyone (other than my wife) to know how much I'm giving to God. This is a very personal thing.

Ten percent is an ancient arbitrary number. Give more than ten percent and you will receive more. Give less and you will receive less. It is done according to your belief.

12.   There really are no wealth secrets.

There are only simple principles that must be maintained in a responsible manner. God only lets the people
who can be a good managers of wealth, receive more
wealth. God is a loving God. Can you imagine him
burdening anyone with more money if they can't handle
what they have already? It is your responsibility to
become the type of person who can handle money
properly. Accumulating wealth is like building a house.
Build a solid foundation of knowledge and faith a little
every day and soon you will have a large, solid, structure. This structure will stand to protect you, as well as
bring great pleasure into your life.

Alice in Wonderland, by Lewis Carroll, contains a very
profound dialogue between Alice and the Red Queen.
When Alice tells the Queen that one cannot believe
impossible things, the Queen replies that Alice probably
has not had much practice. She tells Alice that she
always believed impossible things for half an hour a
day, and that sometimes she has believed as many as six
impossible things before breakfast! If you start believing in impossible things before breakfast, by dinner
time they are not so impossible anymore!

One of my favorite comic strips is *Cathy*, written by
Cathy Guisewite, who said, "All parents believe their
children can do the impossible. They thought it the
minute we were born, and no matter how hard we've
tried to prove them wrong, they all think it about us
now. And the really annoying thing is, they're probably
right."

Chapter 7 Review
Beliefs

1. Beliefs are the filters through which money is accumulated.

2. To better your life and increase prosperity, change your beliefs.

3. The wealthy have different beliefs than the average person.

4. To change your beliefs, you must make a decision to change and act on that decision.

5. Common beliefs of wealthy people are:

    * Attitude is everything.
    * You must face your fears.
    * Go in the opposite direction of most people.
    * All opportunities are disguised as problems.
    * Valuable things can be disguised as worthless.
    * Live by the Golden Rule.
    * Money is attracted to great ideas.
    * You are your own wealth.
    * Networking saves legwork.
    * Establish the habit of success.
    * Share your wealth.
    * There aren't any wealth secrets.

CHAPTER 8

FALSE BELIEFS OF THE UNSUCCESSFUL

THE GREATEST DISCOVERY
OF MY GENERATION IS THAT
HUMAN BEINGS CAN ALTER
THEIR LIVES BY ALTERING
THEIR ATTITUDES OF MIND.

WILLIAM JAMES

*

DO NOT LOOK WHERE YOU
FELL, BUT WHERE YOU
SLIPPED

AFRICAN PROVERB

Just as there are beliefs common to the wealthy, there are false beliefs common to those who are unsuccessful in creating wealth. These false beliefs prevent an individual from accumulating wealth and success. They are passed down from generation to generation without any merit or reason. In an attempt to keep the poor entrenched in poverty, some groups even try to promote these false beliefs.

There are nine false beliefs and they are:

* Having a good job ultimately leads to wealth.
* Saving your money is a good investment.
* Debt is bad, you want to avoid it.
* Security is good and risk is bad.
* Failure is bad.
* Wealth is measured by material possessions.
* The government, your employer or some other person is responsible for your financial well being.
* Acquiring wealth is a win/lose game.
* It takes money to make money.

Let's take a moment and expand on these false beliefs.

1.   Having a good job ultimately leads to wealth.

A job is simply a temporary inconvenience on your way to wealth. If you like your work, you might want to continue doing it after you become wealthy. The choice will be yours after you are financially independent. You must do the best job that you can for your employer, and in return you will increase your integrity and improve your inner person. If you don't like your present job, consider setting a date at which time you will have accumulated enough money so you can resign.

Another important consideration about a job is this—do not be afraid to work. If you're trying to accumulate money, you might need to get a second or third job. Remember this is a *temporary* situation. You might have to be willing to work extra jobs for one, two or even three years to pay off all of your bills, invest and become financially independent. That's a very small price to pay to be able to financially support your dreams for the rest of your life!

Work is part of any wealth accumulation process. Don't be afraid of burning out from overworking. I'd rather burnout than rust-out. You can rest when you become wealthy, but for now be willing to work!

Hallei hired me as a consultant on his path to becoming a billionaire. He already owns over two hundred Dairy Queens and is worth about one hundred seventy-five million dollars. Hallei, his wife and son were all hard workers. Since they had started with nothing in India, they realized that if they were going to accumulate any amount of wealth, work was going to be a part of it. All of them share the dream of accumulating one billion dollars, and they all work 363 days out of the year at their Dairy Queen stores. In addition to their wealth, their son has a structural engineering degree from an ivy league college.

This family does not need to work. However, they share a strong purpose that propels them toward accumulating that kind of wealth. They envision helping the poor in their native land. It was a pleasure to work with this family as they learned many new lessons along their path to wealth. Within six months of hiring me, they acquired an additional twenty-five million dollars.

2.   *Saving your money is a good investment.*

Millionaires are not created by saving's accounts! Don't save every nickel—you must *invest!* Invest in yourself and investment vehicles that bring high returns! Short range investments such as interest bearing money market funds, certificates of deposit and savings accounts are fine, but branch out of these into better wealth producing vehicles as soon as possible. Nobody ever achieved wealth by merely saving. In fact, saving money rather than investing it, is a sure way to prevent wealth accumulation. You must take at least 10% of everything you earn and invest it as soon as possible. I'll cover this in more detail in a later chapter.

3.   *Debt is bad-you must avoid it.*

Only consumer debt is bad. You must avoid that. However, investment debt *(leverage)* is good, and should be used to accelerate your accumulation of wealth. The only temporary consumer debt I would consider having is a home mortgage. After purchasing your home with a mortgage, you need to accelerate your payments to the lender. Debt for investing (real estate, stock margin accounts, and so on) is necessary to accumulate large sums of money. Business and investment debt is actually good for all serious minded wealth seekers.

4.   *Security is good and risk is bad.*

Our entire society is obsessed with security. We demand unemployment security, social security, plus job security and we take out insurance for everything. Relying on an almost insolvent Social Security system will not make you financially secure! The more you need security, the more you avoid risk. You cannot hate risk and hope for financial freedom. Risk is the price you must pay for wealth. You take risks everyday just to stay alive. Although I encourage all wealth seekers to take risks, I suggest you learn the various subjects dealing with money, investments and taxes so your risks will be *educated* risks.

As an educated risk taker, if you lost everything today, you would be able to get back all the lost things (including money) in a matter of two to three years. This is the same for everyone, regardless of your present financial situation. The reason you would be able to recover everything in a fraction of the time is because your present consciousness created your current lifestyle in the first place. You don't need to relearn those lessons. You have already paved the way for yourself. Now you must work to expand your beliefs and realities beyond your current state. Do not become so attached to your current state that you are not willing to risk losing it in order to grow. After all, what do you have to lose? Nothing, because you can get all of it back in a very short period of the time.

Henry Ford was once asked what he would do if he lost all of his possessions. He replied that he would have them all back within five years. How did he know that? Because while building his fortune, he internalized the lessons and basic wealth building principles necessary to build it in the first place. Once the trail has been blazed, it is not necessary to re-blaze it. Once you incorporate the basic principles of wealth into your life, and are not afraid to use them, you will always be wealthy.

5.   Failure is bad.

Failure is simply a learning tool. You should analyze all failures using this question: "What can I learn from this experience?" There is no need to be ashamed of failures in business or in your life. Failure is necessary for success. Successful people usually have many more failures than successes, but they keep going. You do not drown by falling in the water. You drown by staying there.

Failure is not bad. One good failure can teach you more about success than four years at the best university. In fact, there is an elite business school in Texas that requires its professors to have failed in business at least three times before they can become a faculty member!

6.   Wealth is measured by material possessions.

Most millionaires in the world live frugally. They are very conservative with their money and that is why they have it. Material possessions are just the appearance of wealth. They are the form of wealth, but not the substance. Real wealth is measured by the quality of your thoughts, not your things. You can be wealthy without having lots of things, or you can be rich and not be wealthy.

Although this may sound a little confusing, it is really a crucial point. Wealth is a state of mind—an attitude. Wealthy people possess a certain attitude. They do not appear rich when they start accumulating wealth. They accumulate their possessions after they become wealthy in their own minds. By concentrating on their purpose in life and their goals, the wealthy person attracts riches to themselves. It is done from the inside out.

7. The government, your employer or another person is responsible for your financial security.

Believing in this myth will only leave you penniless and stripped of self-respect. Do not lie to yourself thinking you had no other choice in life because that would truly be a waste of time and energy. No one is responsible to bail you out or support you except yourself. A person or event in life cannot truly victimize you unless you allow it to continue. That is a choice you make. The sooner you accept that you alone have total responsibility for yourself, the faster you will be motivated to make the decision to change your circumstances and start to accumulate wealth. Nobody is responsible for giving you anything. Adopt the attitude that you don't want one penny more than you earned.

8. Acquiring wealth is a win/lose game.

Only truth will stand in both life and finance. Truth is based on a win/win outcome. You do not have to cheat or steal from other people to gain wealth and riches. There is an abundance for all who are willing to put forth the necessary effort. The infinite source of wealth has enough for everyone.

Wealth is like air. Are you afraid to breathe the air because you might use it all up? Or take it away from someone else? When you breathe, you are not stealing your neighbor's oxygen. There is an abundance of air around the planet, and more is created everyday. The same is true of wealth. All people can be wealthy. Since wealth is God-made, all people have access to it. It is as simple as a decision to learn how to do it.

9.   *It takes money to make money.*

You can use other people's money to make your money. If your intentions are sincere, others will be able to sense your honesty and determination. In turn, other people will be willing to let you work with their money or credit (not consumer credit) to help you, and them, make more money.

To be in exchange, you have to be willing to give something toward the project. Your contribution could be in preparation, managing, research, and so on. Then perhaps another person would be willing to financially back you in a viable business venture or investment. People sometimes think that luck has something to do with making money. You must replace luck thinking with preparation. Luck does not exist! What appears to be luck is really "opportunity meeting preparation." Believing in luck is like believing in Santa Claus and the Easter Bunny. The concept is nice, but a real person has to deliver the presents. Prepare yourself well to attain your goals. Along the way to achieving your goals, you will be ready for the opportunities as they present themselves. Remember when you take action the energy of the Universe is set in motion for you and the opportunities you seek will come. Wealthy people believe they create their own luck. They create luck by deciding what they want (purpose), writing out a plan (goals), and then taking action. The wealthy seldom buy lottery tickets and only gamble for entertainment.

To create your own luck is another way of saying you want to create a change in your life. Although this seems simple enough, most people quit just before taking this step. The ego kicks in and says, "I like myself the way I am and I am not going to change for anything or anyone, including money. I should be able to get more money just the way I am." Don't misunderstand me; the ego is a vital necessity to maintain life at the human level. People have been trying to control it since the beginning of time. Although the ego has an important function in our lives, problems can occur if we do not control this magnificent power. "Ego taming" is a lifetime job, and there have been literally thousands of techniques developed to keep it in check. Don't allow your ego to keep you from changing your current beliefs and attitudes about money. Since money is nothing more than thought or spiritual energy, if we curb our ego (not get rid of it), we can harnass its amazing power to create the changes we need in order to handle more money in our lives.

Chapter 8 Review
False Beliefs of the Unsuccessful

1. The false beliefs of the person unsuccessful in accumulating wealth are as follows:

    *   Having a good job ultimately leads to wealth.
    *   Saving your money is a good investment.
    *   Debt is bad, you must avoid it.
    *   Security is good and risk is bad.
    *   Failure is bad.
    *   Wealth is measured by material possessions.
    *   The government, your employer or some other person is responsible for your financial well being.
    *   Acquiring wealth is a win/lose game.
    *   It takes money to make money.

2. Don't count on luck. You are your own luck.

3. Don't try to eliminate the ego. Learn to curb it and use it for your benefit. It is a magnificent power.

CHAPTER 9

PURPOSE — THE MAJOR ENERGY BEHIND ANY SUCCESSFUL LIFE

EVERYTHING IN THE UNIVERSE
HAS A PURPOSE. INDEED, THE
INVISIBLE INTELLIGENCE THAT
FLOWS THROUGH EVERYTHING
IN A PURPOSEFUL FASHION IS
ALSO FLOWING THROUGH YOU.

WAYNE DYER

*

THE PURPOSE OF MAN IS
ACTION.

THOMAS CARLYLE

*

WHEN A MAN DOES NOT KNOW
WHAT HARBOR HE IS MAKING FOR,
NO WIND IS THE RIGHT WIND.

SENECA

In order to become successful, you must first create a purpose or mission for your life. When you have found or created your purpose, you can then concentrate on your purpose, instead of your life.

Many people would like to concentrate on their purpose, but they have had difficulty discovering what it's supposed to be. Here is an exercise containing three simple steps to help you to discover your purpose.

Step #1 — *The Purpose Finder Exercise*

Read the following directions. Then stop reading and take a few minutes to do this simple paper and pencil exercise.

Part 1: Divide a blank sheet of paper into four quadrants, and list the following four questions, one in each quadrant left to right.

* What do I love to do?
* What am I good at?
* What is important or essential to me for my life to be complete?
* What was I born to do or feel I ought to be doing?

Do not censor or judge any of your answers. Just brainstorm. Simply write down everything that comes to your mind for each question until you run out of ideas.

Part 2: Look at the answers in each quadrant and ask yourself, "If I only had five years left to live, which seven items in each category would I want to definitely accomplish?" Then select the top seven answers to each of the four questions.

Part 3: Select and prioritize the top three answers in each quadrant, and then compare them to each other. The similarities of all twelve answers (three from each quadrant) will weave together a purpose for your life.

Stop reading now and complete this exercise.

Some of you may be surprised at what you found by doing this exercise. If you're on purpose, then goals are secondary. Your purpose in life can be defined as the "big picture." If you set goals in line with your life's purpose, you will happily achieve them with great satisfaction and truly begin to enjoy life. When you are living your life on purpose, you will jump out of bed in the morning with excitement to begin the day. A purposeful life will make you hesitate to go to bed at night. You will want to live your life to the fullest, working on fulfilling your purpose.

When Rachel came to see me, she had been diagnosed as clinically depressed for the past two years. Her medication seemed to have little effect on her condition. While working with this young mother of three children, I asked her, "What is your purpose in life?" She replied that her purpose was to be a good mother to her children, and a good wife to her husband.

While doing the purpose finder exercise, we found that her family was hardly mentioned. She started crying, feeling guilty for not mentioning her children and husband. I explained that this exercise went deeper than the conscious mind, and we were looking at what she really needed to be happy in life. Her purpose revealed that she needed to be a flower shop owner.

I further explained to Rachel, that if she were working in line with her purpose, she would be happier. If she were happier, she would be a better mother and wife. She saw the connection, and immediately felt relieved. As we parted that day, she hugged me and said, "Thank you so much! I feel like I'm free from my own prison." Rachel accepted a job at a florist and learned the business in a matter of months. She applied for and got a small business loan. She now has a very successful floral business, and recently hired her husband as the office manager to help oversee her twenty-two company employees.

Rachel recently wrote me saying she does not have the time or inclination to be depressed because she is having too much fun! She mentioned that her children are happier and everyone is getting along much better. As we change and start living on purpose, we free the people around us to do the same.

Step # 2 — *Write your purpose statement*

Now that you have an idea of your life purpose, the next step is to use the twelve answers from the exercise to write a purpose statement. For example, my purpose statement is, "To take the average person and teach them how to become debt-free and financially independent." Your purpose statement will guide your life. Write a statement that is clear and simple, and makes you feel alive! You can revise this purpose statement as your life unfolds. A purpose is bigger than life. It actually becomes your life.

When you are on purpose, nothing can stop you. When you are not on purpose, anything can and usually will stop you. Stop the reading now, and take a few minutes to write your own purpose statement.

Step #3 — *Attach your purpose to a compelling reason*

If the why is important enough, then the how is never too difficult. Very few of us would purposely hang off of a 1,000 foot cliff. But, if one of our children or someone else we loved was stuck on the ledge, we would not hesitate to hang over that ledge in our best attempt to save them. The *why* is what motivates you to tirelessly live your purpose, as demonstrated by my friend, Hallei, who owns the Dairy Queens and intends to help the poor in India. The *how* to create wealth is easy to understand, but sometimes difficult to apply; especially if the only reason you're starting on this path is to get rich, then your reason isn't powerful enough. You need a deeper reason that will carry you through the hard times. After establishing a purpose for your life, and attaching your purpose to a compelling reason, then it's time to choose goals that will help you live out your purpose.

A 1954 study of graduating seniors at Yale University showed that upon graduation, only 3% had written down specific, concrete goals. Twenty years later, this graduating class was surveyed again. The 3% that had developed the habit of writing down their goals outperformed the other 97% combined. You must write down your goals, or they will be nothing more than daydreams.

Goals should be written in the following increments: Daily, Weekly, Monthly, Six Months, One Year, Five Years, and Ten Years. Just as you would not set out on a trip without planning your route, you want to do the same with your life. Plan your life and then work your plan.

Chapter 9 Review
Purpose—The Major Energy Behind Any Successful
Life

1. Complete the Purpose Finder exercise.

2. Write your purpose statement.

3. Attach your purpose to a compelling reason. Ask yourself why you are doing your work.

CHAPTER 10

FIVE PARTS
TO
SETTING GOALS

WHETHER OR NOT YOU REACH
YOUR GOALS IN LIFE DEPENDS
ENTIRELY ON HOW WELL YOU
PREPARE FOR THEM AND HOW
BADLY YOU WANT THEM. YOU
ARE EAGLES! STRETCH YOUR
WINGS AND FLY TO THE SKY!

RONALD McNAIR

*

GOALS ARE DREAMS WITH
DEADLINES

DIANA SCHARF HUNT

*

IF YOU WANT TO ACCOMPLISH THE
GOALS OF YOUR LIFE, YOU HAVE TO
BEGIN WITH THE SPIRIT

OPRAH WINFREY

S etting goals is a crucial aspect of wealth accumulation. In order to set goals, you must:

1. Write a personal inventory.

Your personal inventory should include a list of your strengths and weaknesses, time constraints and support from family or friends. Write out all of your resources which might help you to achieve your goals.

2. State your intention.

Your intention is not your goal, it's your purpose or mission statement, which is driven by a deep and meaningful spiritual or inner purpose. Goals are more superficial. They are action steps that give concrete form to your deeper intention.

3. Make an action plan.

Write out a detailed plan to achieve your goals. Attach target dates to each step. Your target dates can be revised, but it is important to state them to keep yourself focused. The more detailed your plan, the faster you will achieve your goals. Break down the larger tasks into smaller ones and then write the smaller steps on a calendar. Now you will have target dates to accomplish the smaller tasks which will ultimately lead to you achieving your goal.

4. Flood your imagination with pictures.

Use visualization. When the will comes into conflict with the imagination, the imagination always wins. Be very detailed with your visualization process. At least daily (and more if possible), find a quiet place and visualize exactly who you are becoming and what you are accomplishing. With your eyes closed, visualize your purpose and goals with as much emotion as you can. Incorporate all six senses—touch, smell, sight, sound, taste and "intuition"—into your visualization. Let your imagination and your heart be your guide. Make your goals and purpose come alive during these visualization sessions. Use your intuition to see more clearly the person you know you can become. The more sessions you give yourself, the faster you will accomplish your goals. Don't substitute visualization for action. Both are meant to be used together for maximum results.

Visualization is an important training tool used by athletes. They can improve their performance simply by visualizing themselves practicing their sport! The most important times to visualize are when you first wake up in the morning, and just before you drift off to sleep at night. At these times, the conscious mind is quiet, and you can directly access your subconscious mind. The subconscious mind is where all internal changes occur. Then you will witness miracles in your physical world!

One very powerful visualization technique is to use what I call a "play prayer." Sit in front of a mirror for at least three minutes daily. Look into your eyes and talk to your reflection as if you have already acquired your goal. For example, if you want to acquire one million dollars, tell yourself what your day was like the day before, what it is going to be like today, now that you are a millionaire, and what it will be like tomorrow. Since you are dealing with your life, be sincere when doing this exercise.

After doing this technique, you should notice how different you feel. You'll actually *feel* like a millionaire (or whatever it was that you wanted to accomplish). The mind will create the necessary power for you to handle your new wealth. Guess what? Your mind will not know if you are playing or if you are for real!

Another visualization technique that works well is to create an imaginary Board of Directors. The people on your Board can be alive or dead, real or fictional. Choose several people of diverse backgrounds that you admire greatly, and bring them into your visualization. Ask them questions and imagine them giving you advice. Really listen to what they tell you. When you are done visualizing, either record or write down the information your Board of Directors gave you.

For instance, my board of directors consists of John F. Kennedy, Benjamin Franklin, Albert Einstein, Plato, Alexander The Great, Abraham Lincoln, Ghandi, Siddhartha Gautama (The Buddha), Jesus Christ, and Henry Kissinger. When I have a problem and can't find a solution, I simply find a quiet place, close my eyes, and visualize myself sitting with these great people. As I tell my Board of Directors my problem, I ask them what their solution would be. Then, using my imagination, I *see and hear* my Board members giving me advice. You'll be amazed at the direction you'll receive from your imaginary Board of Directors meeting.

I have taught this technique to a number of people in my life, but a man named John was the most memorable. He was a thirty-four year old husband and father, who hired me for consultation on his ailing record store. The sales had been steadily dropping over the past three years and he was barely keeping the doors open. As we went over his purpose, we found that he was in the right business. Next, we established his unique selling advantages over his competitors. John still felt that something was missing. I told John about my imaginary Board of Directors and how I use them in my own businesses. We then took an hour off for lunch. As we resumed our session, John was extremely enthusiastic. He had used his lunch hour to work with his own imaginary Board of Directors, and they had given him some great ideas. We spent the afternoon formulating the ideas received from his imaginary Board of Directors. Some of John's ideas were very impressive. John continues to use the advice of his imaginary Board, and his business has grown substantially.

One other important item worth mentioning in visualization techniques is affirmations. Affirmations are the fuel that keep you moving toward your goals. Write an affirmation to yourself, or create a commercial about yourself. Talking to myself with sincere enthusiasm, my commercial might go something like this, "Mike, you are a powerful and committed speaker. You are a teacher of thousands! You have a vast amount of knowledge that can help people change their lives and fulfill their dreams! Every time you help even *one* person become more prosperous, the entire world becomes a better place for everyone!" At first you may feel awkward because you think that it sounds boastful, but affirmations ignite *passion*. Passion fuels *action!* And remember, action brings *empowerment* and *opportunities*. Just make sure you are prepared to accept those opportunities when they come!

Use affirmations every morning just as you wake up, and every evening just before falling asleep so your goals become real and embedded in your subconscious mind.

5. Take at least one small action step daily.

Make certain that you take at least one small step every day toward your goals, intention, or purpose. Do not let a day go by without taking at least one small step that will get you closer to creating your goals or purpose in life. Many would-be successful people have everything they need to achieve success, except they do not go into action. The worst thing you can do is fail to act. Affirmation without action is nothing more than a daydream. Daydreams alone will not put food on your table, clothes on your back or money in your investment portfolio.

Many people convince themselves to wait until they can take giant steps toward their purpose. After twenty or thirty years of waiting for that giant step, they realize how much time they have wasted, and how little time remains in which to accomplish their purpose. Do not let that happen to you! There is an old Chinese proverb that says, "The journey of a thousand miles begins with one step." Take it *now!*

Chapter 10 Review
Five Parts to Setting Goals

There are five parts to writing goals:

1. Write a personal inventory.

2. State your intention.

3. Make an action plan.

4. Flood your imagination with pictures. Create an imaginary Board of Directors with whom you consult regularly.

5. Take at least one small action step daily.

CHAPTER 11

WEALTH-BUILDING SKILLS THAT BREAK THE MONEY BARRIERS AND CREATE MILLIONS

IF YOU HAVE BUILT CASTLES IN THE
AIR, YOUR WORK NEED NOT BE LOST;
THAT IS WHERE THEY SHOULD BE. NOW
PUT FOUNDATIONS UNDER THEM.

HENRY DAVID THOREAU

*

A MAN WITH A SURPLUS CAN
CONTROL CIRCUMSTANCES; BUT
A MAN WITHOUT A SURPLUS IS
CONTROLLED BY THEM , AND
OFTEN HAS NO OPPORTUNITY
TO EXERCISE JUDGMENT.

HARVEY S. FIRESTONE

*

A JUG FILLS DROP BY DROP.

THE BUDDAH

I f your household income is $35,000 per year, in thirty years you will have earned more than one million dollars. The only problem is that most people spend it all! According to the census bureau, 25% of the households in this country live below the poverty level earning less than $10,000 per year. Less than 75% earn $50,000 per year, and only 2.5% earn over $100,000 per year. Why is it that only a very small percentage of people earn ten times or more than the rest of us? It is because they have learned that the process of accumulating money is a system based on the following two skills: learning the value of money and learning how to manage your money.

1.   Learning the value of money.

Learn how to value *every* dollar that flows through your life. Saving just a dollar a day can make you a million-aire. Do not waste even one dollar! Every dollar is a seed for more money.

A one-time investment of a single dollar into a vehicle that pays 3% annual interest will earn you one million dollars in 468 years—a little slow for most of us! If you invest one dollar *per day* at 3% interest, it will grow into a million dollars in 147 years. If you change the interest rate from 3% to 5% annually, you'll make that million dollars in about 100 years. Changing the interest rate to 10% cuts the time to about 56 years. If you change the interest rate to 20%, it cuts the time to about 20 years with that same dollar per day investment! So, investing one dollar per day at 20% annual interest will generate one million in 20 years.

If you invested a dollar a day from the day you were born until you reached retirement age (about 25,000 days) you would have $25,000. At 3% interest, you would have $75,000. At 5% interest you would have $200,000. At 10% interest, you would have $2,500,000. At 15% interest, you would have $50,000,000. At 20% annual interest, you would have one billion dollars! All of this from one dollar per day!

If you put away $10 dollars a day, that's about $3,500 per year, at 20% annual interest you could become a millionaire in less than twenty years! The secret to making one dollar turn into millions or even billions is called *compound interest,* which Einstein called the eighth wonder of the world. When you start saving money for investments on a regular basis, be sure to invest at the beginning of the month instead of the end. You will get an extra month of compound interest moving you toward financial independence.

If you take $200 per month, that's about $2,400 per year, and set a goal for it to grow at 20% per year, in twenty years you'll have $632,000. If you wait just one year to begin saving, in nineteen years you'll end up with only $516,000. That is a $116,000 loss! In other words, you lost over $300 a day by waiting! Every hour you delay you throw away about $13. Every hour you wait is costing you money!

When it comes to saving pennies, this is one time it's better to think small instead of big. Some ask if you have to be a penny pincher to become rich. Not in the negative sense, but you do have to learn to *appreciate and respect* every penny. Be reluctant to let your money go because you love it—you know the potential it has for good works, and the opportunities it affords you.

You must use the technique of delayed gratification if you want to become wealthy. You have to avoid impulsive spending without planning. You must consciously plan every expense. Delayed gratification will help you avoid picking the fruit off your money tree before it ripens. Delayed gratification will make you wealthy, and then you can buy whatever your heart desires. You will need to keep track of every penny you spend. You should carry a journal, such as a check register from the bank, to list all of your cash expenditures daily. This will let you know exactly where you are spending your money.

Many people I consult with are afraid of money. Contrary to what you may have heard or read, it is okay to love money, as long as you keep that love in perspective and balance it ethically in your life. Zig Zigler is well-known and respected the world over as a motivational speaker. He says those who claim the love of money is the root of all evil just flat out don't have any. Though it sounds comical, perhaps that saying has some truth to it.

2. Learning to manage your money.

Many wealthy families teach their children to manage money at a very young age. The Rockefeller children were given an allowance of 25 cents a week. They had to earn any additional money they felt they needed. They were required to keep a log of all their spending, which Mr. Rockefeller reviewed with them on a regular basis. They were directed to give 10% to God, keep 10% for themselves for spending, and to invest the rest. What a marvelous lesson for ourselves as well as our children! We will explore money management in the next chapter.

Chapter 11 Review
Wealth-Building Skills that Break the Money Barriers and Create Millions

1. The first wealth-building skill is to learn to value money.

2. The second wealth-building skill is to learn to manage your money effectively.

CHAPTER 12

MANAGE AND CATEGORIZE TO SAVE A BUNDLE

I COULDN'T WAIT FOR SUCCESS,
SO I WENT AHEAD WITHOUT IT.
NOTHING WILL WORK UNLESS
YOU DO.

JOHN WOODEN

*

E ARN AS MUCH AS YOU CAN.
SAVE AS MUCH AS YOU CAN.
INVEST AS MUCH AS YOU CAN.
GIVE AS MUCH AS YOU CAN.

REV. JOHN WELLESLY

*

N O ONE IS FREE WHO IS NOT LORD
OVER HIMSELF.

CLAUDIUS

H ere are ten effective habits that most, if not all, wealthy people have developed in themselves:

1.   *Live below your current income to create a surplus of money.*

Part of learning to manage your money effectively is learning to live below your current income. Starting today, make a real commitment to live below your means to help you create a surplus which you can invest. Think of money as water filling up a bathtub. If you are filling up the bathtub, but do not have the drain plugged, you will not be very successful. Plug that drain! Then find more faucets!

2.   *Keep track of every penny.*

This can feel burdensome at first until you develop the habit, but it's a prerequisite to taking charge of your finances. Did you know that the average wealthy person usually spends about 30 to 60 seconds longer in the grocery store line because they list the expense category on their receipt?

To manage your money successfully, set up the following ten categories and monitor these on a daily basis:

* Reciprocal Maintenance (wherever you receive spiritual sustenance)
* Self
* Taxes
* Housing
* Personal (this is the largest category and includes whatever it costs you to live. For example, food, clothes, housing repairs, etc.)

* Auto (car payments, insurance, gas, repairs)
* Entertainment (include vacations)
* Insurance (health, life, disability, etc.)
* Miscellaneous (include debts)
* Business

Additional categories are not necessary. Since most of us spend money only a few times a day, categorizing the expenditures at the checkout line, keeping track of the receipts and then keeping a running total of the categories on a daily basis will ensure that you stay within your budget.

This simple process can make the difference between wealth and poverty. Do not buy impulse items. Only buy the items that you planned to purchase before you entered the store.

3. Spend your money the way wealthy people do.

* Decide exactly what you are going to buy before you enter the store.
* Compare prices in order to take advantage of potential savings. Don't be afraid to ask for a discount.
* Check each receipt for accuracy, and put it in a safe place for filing later.
* Write down the purchase and categorize it into one of the ten categories.

This may take you an extra minute, but you will lower your cost of spending by 20% to 30% annually. This could be called the millionaire's minute because it is exactly how millionaires manage their money. If you incorporate this habit into your life, you can become a millionaire.

When a wealthy person comes home, they immediately record their expenditures and file their receipts. This will also help you save money on your taxes. Remember you want cash flow *management*. You must increase the inflow and decrease the outflow.

4.   Wealthy people love to save money. Here's a few of the most important ways they do it:

*   Buy wholesale or discounted items whenever you can.
*   Learn to invest your money at high wealth-producing rates of return.
*   Destroy all your credit cards, except one for true emergencies. This should immediately cut your expenses by 20% to 30% per month and will help eliminate impulse buying.
*   Reduce the amount of money you carry in your pocket. This will help cut down impulse buying.

5.   Know how to invest your money. Make it grow at least 20 - 30% MONTHLY.

This wealth building skill involves knowing how to invest your money at wealth-producing rates of return. Anyone can make their money grow at 3%, but you must learn how to make your money grow at 20 to 30% MONTHLY! Wealthy people do this every day! If you want to become wealthy, you must accept responsibility for learning how to do the same. You can learn about money management and investments by going to seminars, reading books and periodicals, listening to tapes and talking to other people. Books opened a whole new world of investment ideas for me, which changed my finances forever. I changed my thinking from 10% to 15% annually to 20 to 30% monthly.

Ernest Haskins said, "Save a little money each month and at the end of the year, you'll be surprised at how little you have." He's right! Don't save; you must *invest* and do so at wealth-producing rates of return.

6.   Start your own business.

Still another wealth building skill is knowing how to make money. This is a different skill than investing. Investing is passive because someone else does the work for you. An example would be a bank account. Making money is the entrepreneurial side of money. The fastest growing industry in the United States is the home business sector.

There are many benefits to having a business in your home. You are your own boss and you receive great tax breaks, which I'll elaborate on later. Every person in America needs to own their own business.

Here are some basic guidelines for starting your own business.

* Start a business that is in line with your purpose.
* Decide on your ideal lifestyle, then choose a business that will get you there.
* Become the best in your chosen field.
* Ride a trend that is on the rise, not declining.
* Copy others. Don't be the first to try something radical. Much can be learned from other's mistakes that will save you time and money.
* Be slow to hire. Keep employees to a minimum.
* Constantly economize.

*   Avoid overhead like a disease. A new desk or
computer is unnecessary unless it is going to
make you more money immediately.

**7.   Keep your present job and still have a part-time
business for tax breaks and extra income.**

I have been in business for myself since I was eight
years old. Most people would not hire an eight year old.
I had no choice but to start my own business if I wanted
to change our circumstances. I've had lots of time to
reflect on my mistakes, and I still believe that being in
business for yourself is one of the best ways to become
wealthy. Remember, you can keep your present job and
still have a part-time business that gives you tax breaks
and extra income. Research this at the library, or take a
tax course to give you the information you need. Your
extra income can be used to pay off your bills, or to
invest in income generating vehicles.

**8.   Shield your money effectively using corpora-
tions, trusts and partnerships.**

Another skill you must develop is the ability to effectively shield or protect your money. To make it is one
thing, but to keep it is quite another. Lawsuits are at an
all time high. Learn how to utilize corporations, trusts
and partnerships to protect your assets. If you are
accumulating wealth, there's almost a 100% chance you
will be sued. Don't be intimidated by this. Just be smart
and protect yourself against this possibility.

Make sure your corporations, trusts and partnerships
own your assets, and that you own those entities. Books
on this subject are plentiful, and some even contain the
proper forms to be filled out and filed. Many of these
entities are very simple to establish. For example, you

can incorporate a business yourself for about $100, or pay an attorney $1,000.

Even if you hire an attorney to do the paperwork, it is your responsibility to learn how to start and maintain a trust or corporation. This will let you know if the person that you hired is doing their job right. I've caught many attorneys, and other well-meaning, intelligent professionals making major mistakes with my money simply because I took the time to do a little studying beforehand. You don't have to become an attorney, accountant, or stockbroker; just know the basics.

9. *Ten rules to live by for financial protection.*

To protect your money there are many rules you will learn on your own. I have ten personal rules that I live by, which are:

* Avoid putting assets in your name.
* Never co-sign a loan for anyone.
* Carry adequate liability insurance.
* Do not serve on a Board of Directors.
* Avoid all recourse (personally liable debt).
* Operate all business from a corporate entity or trust.
* Do not go into business without a business plan.
* Do not enter into a partnership without a foolproof way of getting out.
* Diversify only after you start making money.
* Plan for the worst, but expect the best.

10. Share your money. Remember reciprocal maintenance.

You must share your money. Historically, the reason most wealthy parents teach their children to give 10% to God is because they regard all money as belonging to God anyway. They simply view themselves as the caretakers of God's money. Since the money belongs to God, they are happy to give back at least 10%.

Look for ways to give your money and unwanted material things away. Clean out your house and give the excess to the needy. You will feel better, and get a nice tax break, although as we discussed earlier that should not be your primary motivation. Most importantly, you will be in the flow for more money to come into your life.

Remember that this flow or cycle called reciprocal maintenance states that you must give back to wherever it is that you are receiving your spiritual sustenance. If you stop giving, whatever you are receiving will stop flowing to you. Farming is a good example of reciprocal maintenance. Farmers plant crops and give back to their fields on a regular basis by providing fertilizer, water and attention as needed. After several months, the farmer receives his harvest.

What would happen if the farmer did not participate in reciprocal maintenance with his fields? What if he just planted a crop and walked away, never giving anything back? He would come back in just a short period of time to find very little to harvest and his fields full of weeds.

If you are not receiving an abundant crop of money, examine how much you are giving away. Start giving a percentage of your income to wherever you receive spiritual support and guidance. It could be a church, a favorite organization, a friend who emotionally supports you, a waiter who gives you extra attention, or to your favorite park. There are many places and people who fill you with joy if you will just take the time to notice. From your heart, start giving away a percentage of the money you receive. You will be amazed at the response, both emotionally and financially.

Chapter 12 Review
Manage and Categorize to Save Bundle

1. Live below your current income to create a surplus of money.

2. Keep track of every penny you spend.

3. Spend your money the way wealthy people do:

    *   Decide exactly what you are going to buy before you enter the store.
    *   Compare prices in order to take advantage of potential savings.
    *   Ask a clerk for a discount.
    *   Check each receipt for accuracy, immediately categorize it and put it in a safe place for filing later.
    *   When you get home, record the purchase in one of the ten categories and keep cumulative totals to make sure you are staying within your budget.

4. Wealthy people love to save money. Here are a few of the most important ways to do it:

    *   Buy wholesale or discounted items as much as possible.
    *   Learn to invest your money at high wealth producing rates of return.
    *   Destroy all your credit cards, except one for true emergencies. This should cut your expenses by 20% to 30% per month, and will help eliminate impulse buying.
    *   Reduce the amount of money you carry in your pocket.

5. Know how to invest your money. Make your money grow at 20% to 30% MONTHLY! Accept responsibility for learning about investments that have wealth-producing rates of return. This is accomplished by going to seminars, reading books and periodicals, listening to tape series and talking to other people.

6. Start your own business.

   * Find a business that is in agreement with your purpose.
   * Decide on your ideal lifestyle, and then choose a business that will get you there.
   * Become the best in your chosen field.
   * Ride a trend that is on the rise, not declining.
   * Copy others. Do not be the first to try something radical.
   * Be slow to hire. Keep the number of your employees to a minimum.
   * Constantly economize.
   * Avoid overhead like a disease.

7. Remember, you can keep your present job and still have a part-time business that will give you tax breaks and extra income.

8. Effectively shield your money. You must learn how to protect your money; how to set up corporations, trusts and partnerships to protect your assets, and then, own those entities.

9. Ten rules to live by for financial protection:

   * Avoid putting assets in your name.
   * Never co-sign a loan for anyone.

* Carry adequate liability insurance.
* Do not serve on a Board of Directors.
* Avoid all recourse (personally liable debt).
* Operate all business from a corporate entity or trust.
* Do not go into business without a business plan.
* Do not enter into a partnership without a fool proof way of getting out.
* Diversify only after you start making money.
* Plan for the worst, but expect the best.

10. Share your money. Remember reciprocal maintenance.

CHAPTER 13

SEVEN PRINCIPLES
WEALTHY PEOPLE
HAVE IN COMMON

THE PERSON WHO GOES FARTHEST IS USUALLY THE ONE WHO IS WILLING TO DO AND DARE. THE SURE-THING BOAT NEVER GETS FAR FROM SHORE.

DALE CARNEGIE

*

HISTORY DEMONSTRATES THAT THE MOST NOTABLE WINNERS USUALLY ENCOUNTERED HEARTBREAKING OBSTACLES BEFORE THEY TRIUMPHED. THEY WON BECAUSE THEY REFUSED TO BECOME DISCOURAGED BY THEIR DEFEATS.

B. C. FORBES

*

WEALTH IS A PRODUCT OF MAN'S CAPACITY TO THINK.

AYN RAND

Although there are many principles that wealthy people utilize in their everyday lives, I have found seven they have in common. They live by these guidelines in order to attain their wealth, and to keep it once they get it:

1. *Don't count your dollars until you have paid your taxes and expenses.*

After paying your taxes and expenses, then you have your real money. This tells you where you are financially, and gives you a realistic working budget. When I started working with Dr. George, an orthopedic surgeon, he could not figure out why he was not wealthy. He was making over a million dollars a year in his practice, but his personal bills were eating him alive. As we went over his business and personal budgets and his tax information, we found that Dr. George's take home pay was about $38,000 a year. After our work together, Dr. George's annual take home pay went up to $240,000 a year. He also cut out some of his more elaborate expenses and enrolled in a tax course.

2. *Make maximum use of your assets.*

Invest in things that go up in value. Unfortunately, most of us spend our money on things that make us appear to be wealthy, but in reality these investments lose their value over time. If you are really serious about building wealth, you cannot afford to invest in items that lose value. Remember that most wealthy people use delayed gratification.

When I first met Craig and Cheryl, I quickly realized that their financial problem was one that I had witnessed frequently. Craig and Cheryl were both in their forties and had accumulated over $60,000 in credit card debt alone. As we began our work together, I explained that they needed to stop their impulsive spending. We agreed on a budget that would take care of their necessities, but nothing else. The first thing that was cut from the budget was any frivolous spending. Although this was a scary step, Craig and Cheryl agreed to try it for two years. In less than a year they were able to pay off their credit card debt and had established a habit of investing. At the two year mark, they were happily on their way to becoming financially independent.

3.   Don't diversify too soon.

Mark Twain said it best, "Put all your eggs in one basket and watch that basket." If you are just beginning to accumulate wealth, you must concentrate all your energy on one idea. This is done only at the beginning stage of wealth accumulation. After the money starts rolling in, then naturally, diversification is the next step. In the beginning stages of wealth building, you are a wealth seeker. As a wealth seeker you should invest a small percentage of your assets in low risk investments such as saving accounts or mutual funds. But, put most of your money in high risk investments which produce high returns. If those fail, you can then fall back on your small, low risk investments.

Sam was into six different multilevel marketing programs, had his own consulting business, and worked part-time for an accounting firm. Although he had numerous potential income sources, he was not making much money. I asked Sam to consider letting all of the businesses and his job go, except one. I told him it was only temporary until he started making decent money at the one of his choice.

His purpose finder exercise revealed that his consulting business was the one he should keep. In less than one year, Sam's consulting business had an income in the six figure range. The following year, Sam diversified and started another company that was in line with his consulting firm. This was also a major success. When first starting down your road to seeking wealth, do not diversify. You first need to gain power and momentum within yourself.

4.   *Be on the offense and not on the defense.*

Most of us are overly concerned with security. We do not want to take risks. The problem is that low risk investments do not grow rapidly enough to build a great amount of wealth. In addition to having those safe investments, you must also learn to be assertive and comfortable with risk. Concentrating on security means you have a defensive posture. Taking risk puts you on the offensive. When we are defensive, our lives contract. When we are offensive, our lives expand. If we want to accumulate wealth and grow to our maximum potential, we must stay in the expansion mode.

Throughout nature, growth only occurs when a living entity is expanding. Our mindset determines whether we are offensive (expanding) or defensive (contracting). Negative thoughts cause us to contract in an effort to protect ourselves. Positive thoughts easily help us to expand and receive prosperity. Can you imagine a successful, powerful person slumped over and talking negatively? Of course not! It would be a very rare, short-lived occasion! Powerful, successful people carry themselves with confidence.

5. *Your money must multiply at wealth producing rates of return.*

Wealth producing rates of return depend on your personal goals. If you want to make more money in a shorter period of time, then you need to multiply your money faster. In order to make money multiply faster, you must use leverage, which is another word for credit. Remember, this kind of credit is very different from consumer credit, and is the only kind of credit that is good.

It's impossible to create great wealth without some form of leverage. For example, let's say you buy $1,000 worth of stock in ABC Corporation at $10 per share. This will give you 100 shares of stock. If the stock goes up $1 per share, you'll make $100 or 10% return on your money. If you borrow an additional $1000 (on margin for example), and add this to your original $1000, and the stock goes up $1 per share, you'll make $200. Still, you only have $1000 of your own money invested, and you've made a 20% return on your original $1,000 investment (disregarding the interest on the loan).

Of course, the flip-side of this example is that if the stock goes down, you could lose money. You have to teach yourself to take educated risks in order to establish wealth. This doesn't mean gambling. You must research your investments in order to eliminate as much risk as possible.

6. *Choose investments that are both powerful and stable.*

A perfect investment would be one that you could sell fast, required no management, showed constant growth, had great borrowing power, was protected from inflation and deflation, was a good tax shelter, and generated a steady cash flow. Although you can find investments that contain a number of these qualities, there is no such thing as the perfect investment. However, the more of these qualities an investment has, the better it will be for you.

You must look for both power and stability in an investment. Power means that the investment has a high growth rate achieved by a reasonable use of leverage (borrowing power). Stability means that the investment continues to have an upward growth trend over time. Only certain collectibles, like antiques, art, and real estate would qualify. Money market funds and savings accounts are stable and safe, but are not powerful enough to generate a true wealth-producing rate of return. Commodities are very powerful but notoriously unstable, and can result in rapid losses. Real estate is both powerful and stable, but not liquid. Every investment vehicle has its trade-offs. Yet, there must be another type of sound investment that has great earning potential where the risk, though high, is minimized through adequate research and preparation.

The stock market is a potentially powerful investment tool when combined with margin trading and adequate research. Margin trading is using money borrowed from your stock broker. But, the market can be notoriously volatile. Some of my favorite stock market plays actually use the market's volatility, reducing the risk factor and increasing the rate of return dramatically. These are very powerful plays. I strongly suggest that all serious wealth seekers read my book, *Simple Stock Market,* which covers these plays. If you can't find it please write or call me.

When considering the principle of power and stability, realize that stability is more important than liquidity. Most investment advisors use the "when" investment approach, meaning you should learn when to buy low and then sell high. However, it is often better to use the "how" investment approach. It is not necessarily *when* to buy, but *how* to buy items such as real estate and stocks. There will always be real estate and the stock market, so have no fear about not being able to recover a loss.

7.   Control is essential.

Anytime you hear of someone losing a large amount of money, you will probably find a common thread. In most cases they transferred ultimate control of their money to someone else, who either used bad judgment or was dishonest. The main purpose in sharing this information is to educate and help you make wise financial choices. By studying these principles, you can eliminate the majority of risks involved in accumulating wealth. It has been said that a fool and his money are soon parted. Even though I have made millions, I have also lost millions through a great deal of foolishness. Learn from others' mistakes in order to make the kind of money that you want to make.

You have to be a good manager of your money. People who manage other people have limited power. People who manage money have developed the skills necessary to create and manage anything. Whatever you spend money on is an investment and needs to be managed properly. Think about that the next time you go through the checkout line and see all those impulse items. As a money manager, only choose investments that generate money.

Chapter 13 Review
Seven Principles Wealthy People Have in Common

Prosperous people live by these guidelines in order to attain wealth, and keep it once they get it. These guidelines are as follows:

1. Do not count your dollars until you have paid your taxes and expenses.

2. Make maximum use of your assets. Invest in things that go up in value.

3. Do not diversify too soon.

4. Always be on the financial offense and not on the defense. Most of us are mainly concerned with security. We must learn to take risks. Our mindset is what determines whether we are offensive (expanding) or defensive (contracting).

5. Money must multiply at wealth-producing rates of return. This depends on your personal goals. If you want to make more money in a shorter period of time, then you need to multiply your money faster.

6. Choose investments that are both powerful and stable. Power means that an investment has a high growth rate achieved by the reasonable use of leverage (borrowing power). Stability means that an investment continues to have an upward growth trend over time.

7.   Control of your money is essential. In most cases, if someone has lost a great deal of money, they have probably transferred ultimate control of their money to someone else, who either used bad judgment or was dishonest.

CHAPTER 14

THE
MOST POWERFUL
WEALTH-BUILDING
SECRET IN LIFE

WHEN YOU FACE YOUR FEAR, MOST OF THE TIME YOU WILL DISCOVER THAT IT WAS NOT REALLY SUCH A BIG THREAT AFTER ALL. WE ALL NEED SOME FORM OF DEEPLY ROOTED, POWERFUL MOTIVATION—IT EMPOWERS US TO OVERCOME OBSTACLES SO WE CAN LIVE OUR DREAMS.

LES BROWN

WEAVE IN FAITH. GOD WILL FIND THE THREAD.

PROVERB

A lthough this is one of the shortest chapters in the book, it is by far the most important. According to history, this little secret is how the richest person of his time acquired his fortune.

Thousands of years ago, a great king named Solomon ruled his kingdom with love and fairness. Many people throughout the land, including business associates, friends and family, continuously asked him for advice, wondering how he managed to accumulate such great wealth. After many years of coaxing, King Solomon agreed to share his secret. He sent word to the people throughout the land to gather at the base of a certain mountain on a specific day. This was the day everyone had been waiting for—the moment they too would gain the insight necessary for them to accumulate incredible wealth.

As the massive crowd gathered, they were expecting a long, drawn-out plan. But, the message was very short and direct. At the appointed time, King Solomon walked out to the mountain, climbed to an elevated position, looked out at the crowd and proclaimed, "Save 10% of everything your household earns. Then invest it into a business that makes more money. *Never* touch this money unless you use it to make more money. If you follow these simple steps, great wealth will be yours quickly." The King turned and walked away, though the crowd was plainly upset. Some had traveled for many days to hear this one-minute message. They wanted more! Surely this simple advice from the richest man in the world wasn't complete!

King Solomon stopped, turned to the crowd and said, "That really is all there is to creating great wealth. Do not make it more complicated." Although some in the crowd were bewildered, others tried the King's advice and became wealthy.

The lesson is simple, yet it is crucial and extremely effective—save 10% of the gross income from every-thing you earn and put this money in a separate account called a *money building fund*. This account is known by the wealthy as their principle. The only action you're allowed to take with this money is to invest it. Your money building fund is used *only* to make more money. Eventually this fund will grow into thousands, hundreds of thousands, and ultimately millions! When you reach the point where you can live off the income generated from this money building fund (*unearned income*), you are truly financially independent. Regardless of how much money you make, this fund will grow rapidly along with your wealth. You must start this today, in spite of any indebtedness.

Many people suggest paying all of your bills off first. I do *not* suggest this simply because you must get the momentum of wealth established in your life. Don't add any new bills, and pay off as many debts as fast as possible, but start saving immediately. You will never miss it! Of course, you could put more than 10% into this money building fund, but in order to accumulate any sort of financial independence you *must* first pay yourself 10% of any money coming into your house-hold. You work hard! You deserve it!

The unusual thing about creating a money building fund is noticing how fast it grows. You will find that the money building fund will create momentum in your life towards saving more. This desire to save more will cause the mind to create new income vehicles.

If you are not familiar enough with investments to put this money to work right away in a high yield investment, don't worry. You can start by putting it in a low interest savings account, money market, or certificate of deposit. As the money grows so will your motivation to study more about investments. Your increased studies will result in more knowledge, which will help you find ways to generate higher yields on your cash.

Start today! Put 10% of everything you earn in a money building fund that will move you into financial independence. And remember, don't touch it for anything other than *making more money* by taking well-researched and educated risks.

Chapter 14 Review
The Most Powerful Wealth-Building Secret in Life

This little secret goes back to the days of King Solomon, the wealthiest person of that time:

1. Save 10% of the gross from everything you earn.

2. Put this money in a separate account called a *money building fund*. Invest it at a wealth-producing rates of return. Use this money building fund *only* to make more money.

3. Regardless of how much or little money you make, this fund will grow rapidly. You must start this today, in spite of any indebtedness.

4. Do not wait to start paying yourself. Many people suggest paying off all of your bills first. Pay off as many debts as fast you can, and don't add any new debt, but you *must* start saving 10% today. Put it into your money building fund and make it grow! You deserve it!

CHAPTER 15

PAY OFF
YOUR DEBT

THE PRIVATE CONTROL OF
CREDIT IS THE MODERN FORM
OF SLAVERY.

UPTON SINCLAIR

*

CREDIT BUYING IS MUCH LIKE
BEING DRUNK. THE BUZZ HAPPENS
IMMEDIATELY, AND IT GIVES YOU A
LIFT. THE HANGOVER COMES THE
DAY AFTER.

DR. JOYCE BROTHERS

*

OUT OF DEBT, OUT OF
DANGER.

PROVERB

Once you absorb the information we have covered so far, your entire life will begin changing and you will begin to earn more money. In fact, you will begin to earn vast amounts of money. Once you have money, how do you keep it and make it grow?

According to statistics, 99% of all people living in the United States will never achieve financial freedom. Most people do not even know the exact dollar amount their investments, retirement funds, or social security will generate for them during their retirement years. The government announced last year that Social Security will be completely broke by the year 2005. That means that if you are counting on this money for retirement, it is not going to be there.

Most of us work hard and make a great deal of money during our lifetime. If you think back to ten years ago, you are probably making more money than you ever dreamed possible, but you are not doing any better financially. The American dream of financial independence is not working because the American people have been seduced into borrowing money. No one is responsible for your financial health except you, so you must accept the fact that borrowing money is a scam. Consumer debt is a cancer that will eat away your financial health. Once you accept this fact, you must make *every effort* to learn how to avoid and eliminate consumer debt.

Here are 14 principles that will help you pay off your debt:

1. Lenders are not really on your side. Though the individuals working in these institutions usually have good intentions, any company in the business of lending money is not working for you, even though they will try to make it look that way. Banks, lending institutions, and mortgage companies are organizations that will actually take more than three quarters of all your lifetime income!

2. A mortgage is not a good tax break. When you purchase a home with a mortgage, you will pay back over three times the purchase price. Multiply your monthly payment by the number of months you financed your home! For the average $100,000 house, you'll pay over $300,000 to the mortgage company! This means that you will have paid over $200,000 in interest, just for borrowing the money. That is twice what you borrowed in the first place!

Remember, the government always takes their chunk first. So, to make the $300,000 to pay for your $100,000 home, you really have to make $400,000 to cover the taxes too. That is about a half million dollars just for a $100,000 house! We sweat and bargain for a loan in order to hand them the opportunity to take our money. As you may know, mortgage companies use an amortization schedule, which is to their benefit, plus they charge you closing costs and points on top of the mortgage. If you have an 8% mortgage rate, for example, and your loan is less than ten years old, between 90% and 97% of your monthly payment is interest, which means you really have a 90%-97% interest rate on your property! This is because you are paying between 90%-97% in interest *every month*! Don't fall into the trap of thinking that a home mortgage is a tax break. If you're in the 25% tax bracket, you will get twenty-five cents back on your taxes for every dollar spent on your mortgage. Do not be fooled by this. If you like this type of tax break, just send me the money and I will send you back twenty-five cents on every dollar.

In many areas of the country, real estate is not increasing in value at a substantial rate. Although real estate is a sound investment, it is not a sound investment when you are mortgaged for thirty years. The average American may not be able to save enough money to pay for a house with cash. Go into your mortgage armed with this information. Commit yourself to paying off your mortgage in five to seven years. It is possible, if you stay disciplined and remain focused on achieving your financial independence.

You will pay a little more than three dollars for every dollar borrowed on credit. Even a child with no financial or business knowledge at all will tell you that this is not a good deal! Auto companies are in the business of finance. They make nominal money on the car, and big money on financing. The dealer teaches their sales people to concentrate on finding out how much of a monthly payment you can afford. Then he puts a number of additional charges on top of the sticker price. Most of these charges are considerably marked up. Some of the markups include options (bells and whistles), market adjustment (pure profit), extended warranty, dealer preparation, destination charge, and loan kickbacks from the auto company or bank.

What the car salesman concentrates on is getting you into a car that is within your predetermined monthly payment range, regardless of the total price of the car. That is it! In reality he used the basic American tendency to be concerned only with the monthly payment. The monthly payment consciousness is why auto companies have come out with five and six year car loans. They realize that most people would finance a car for fifty years, if the lending institutions would let them. Why? Because most people aren't aware of the big picture.

It is amazing that the engineers who design cars only design them to last an average of four years. But, if you finance a car for five years, you are gambling against the odds that your car will even run the last year or two. The point I am trying to make is that in order for you to be financially healthy, and to reach financial independence in your lifetime, you must pay off your debt and live only on a cash basis. By doing this, you will own everything you have, and you will not be vulnerable to the credit trap. You will actually live with much less stress, and have the necessary money to invest in wealth producing vehicles.

3. You cannot reach financial independence by using consumer credit. Any kind of credit gives a temporary, false sense of wealth and security. Actually, it can keep you enslaved forever. You can't reach financial independence using consumer credit. You start out with a little bit, then you want more and more. Finally, you are in serious debt. The American people have approximately 15 trillion dollars of consumer debt from using the worst credit drug of them all—the credit card. Get out of the credit card system! Even if you believe you are managing your credit, at 15 to 21% interest you'll end up paying four times the real cost of your purchase. For example, if you put a $2,000 charge on a credit card at 21%, and made the minimal monthly payments required, it would take thirty years to pay off the initial $2,000. You would be paying more than $10,000 total! That's $8,000 interest for borrowing $2000, not to mention the stress of carrying payments for that long. In addition, you would have to earn $13,000 (before taxes) to pay back $10,000. What if you did not make that $2000 charge, and instead invested that $2,000 in a vehicle that yielded 10% interest annually? You would earn over $150,000 in the same amount of time! Is a $2000 purchase worth $158,000? Obviously you would be much better off saving until you had the money to pay cash.

4. Credit is the "opiate of the people." Credit card companies only make money when you are in debt. Now, you can use your credit cards at grocery stores, gas stations, movie theaters, restaurants as well as the television and the internet. Credit has become the "opiate of the people," yet most of the stress in our lives comes from participating in the credit system.

5. Break the credit card addiction. Before you buy, ask yourself why. When considering a purchase, stop and talk to yourself. Ask questions like, "Do I really need this right now? If so, why?" Use delayed gratification.

6. When you accumulate money, you'll buy less. You will find that as you accumulate money, you will want to buy less. Once you experience the power of creating and managing money, frivolous things you used to purchase no longer capture your attention.

7. Overcome the habit of spending impulsively. There are a number of techniques that you can use to overcome spending impulses. Here are just a few:

* Carry only a limited amount of cash.
* Refuse to use credit cards. Cut all of them up except one for true emergencies.
* Agree to use checks, including your ATM card, only for budgeted household expenses (groceries and monthly household bills) and *not* for any other purchases.
* If you need to make a purchase outside your regular monthly household budget, go to the bank and withdraw the money.

* Make it hard on yourself to make an unscheduled or unplanned purchase.
* Agree to a 72 hour waiting period before you purchase any item over $25. Agree not to purchase it for 72 hours after first wanting to buy it.
* If you don't have the full amount of money saved, put it on layaway until you do.
* Start a separate saving fund for an expensive item.
* Stop and ask yourself if this item will help you achieve financial independence. If it will not, but you want it anyway, then list at least five solid reasons why the purchase cannot wait for a few more years until you can truly afford it.
* When you are tempted to finance a purchase, figure out what it is really going to cost you in the end by multiplying the selling price, including tax, times four. You have to use four because you must figure it based on your taxable income.

8. *Make the crucial change to cash.* The most crucial change that you can make is to operate completely on cash. Never use credit again except for true medical emergencies! Most people operating with this information can retire their home mortgage in five to seven years. You will own your home outright, and have the ability to move into a larger house if you choose.

Life is FUN and much less stressful living on a cash-only basis! Look at your whole financial picture—what you have done in the past, what you are doing now, and where you are heading. Since money is so important to each of us, we need to use some smarts about the subject. If you don't pay off your mortgage and creditors quickly, what will you REALISTICALLY have thirty years from now? Include savings, investments and equity in your home. Also, add up your total monthly payments to creditors and include those.

9. Accelerate your payments. *The* next important change you must make is to accelerate your payments. By paying more than your minimum payment, you will retire your financed bills early and save an incredible amount of money in interest. Pay off all debts as quickly as possible.

10. Mark all additional payments "For principal only." When paying bills off in an accelerated manner, make sure the lender knows that the additional money is intended for principal only. Otherwise, it could be applied towards the interest they are charging you. Write two separate checks each month—one for your regular monthly payment, and on the other make a note that it is to be applied directly towards your principal. Now that you understand how the credit industry abuses us, you need to discover how to stop being abused and start actively creating wealth!

11. Discover the magic of the accelerated "roll over" debt elimination system. There are many debt elimination plans that you can follow. The best one that I have found eliminates debt mathematically in a short period of time. The following equation shows how this works:

Creditor balance +
monthly payment amount = order of debt payoff

Here's how to do it: Make a chart listing all your creditors in one column. Put the corresponding balance for each creditor in the column next to that. List the minimum monthly payment each creditor requires in the third column. Determine how many months are left to pay off the balance and put that in the fourth column. Then rank each bill in ascending order starting with the *lowest balance first.*

Creditor	Balance	Pmt	Mos	Rank
Auto	7,100	135	52	5
Doctor	2,700	95	28	3
Discover	875	35	25	1
AmEx	1,875	70	27	2
MBNA	5,500	171	32	4

If you follow this debt elimination plan, your bills will be paid off in the following order:

1) Discover Card—As you keep making the minimum payments on *all* your credit cards, you begin acceleration by collecting *at least* $100 from all the ways that you usually waste money. (Ways to trim your budget are discussed shortly.) Add this $100 to the Discover minimum monthly payment of $35. This brings your total monthly payment to $135. Making a $135 monthly payment decreases the total number of months to retire your Discover debt from 25 months to 6.48 months!

2) AmEx—With Discover paid off, you can now take the $35 monthly payment (from Discover) and your extra $100, and roll it into bill #2—AmEx. You will now be paying $205 a month to AmEx. Since you have already made six months of $70 payments to the AmEx, your total balance is now down to approximately $1,415. You will be able to retire this card in 7 months!

3) Doctor's Office—While you've been accelerating AmEx, you have continued to pay the $95 minimum on this card for thirteen months, bringing the total balance down to $1,465. Now you can roll the $205 from AmEx into this account, plus your minimum monthly payment, making a monthly payment of $300. This account will be paid off in 4.88 months!

4) MBNA—You've been paying the $171 minimum for seventeen months while you have accelerated the above three cards and paid those off. Your MBNA balance is now $2,593. With accelerated payments of $471 ($300 + $171), you will retire this card in 5.5 months!

5) Auto Loan—Your balance after 22 months of the $135 minimum payments you have made while paying off the other four cards, leaves you with a balance on this account of $4,130. Combining $471 and $135 ($606 total), you will retire this debt in 6.8 months!

Using this accelerated "roll over" debt elimination system, you will be completely out of debt in about twenty-eight months, instead of fifty-two—roughly HALF the time!

12. Use the $100 key to freedom. You can use this key to save up for a down payment for a mortgage or to pay off a mortgage. If you wonder where the extra money will come from to use this system, you will be amazed to hear that EVERYONE wastes a substantial amount of money each month. When I sit down with clients I have no trouble trimming a minimum of $100 off their current spending. The best part is they *always* tell me they *never miss it*, and that they feel deeply *empowered* after taking this crucial step.

Calculate your spending for one week: fast food, impulse items at the gas station and grocery store, soda and candy purchases, little extra items from the grocery budget, just to name a few. Magazine subscriptions, video rentals, books, CDs, and so on, most of which can be checked out from the library for free! Inexpensive is great, free is better. Get creative! Choose to spend wisely. Use coupons. Shop sales. You don't have to stop all your spending, just prioritize it so you can find that initial $100 for your debt payoff account. You will use this account to accelerate your debt payoff, one bill at a time. You will not have to live like this forever, only a couple of years and you will be entirely debt free and able to afford to pay cash for whatever you want. Although this may seem difficult at first, you'll find it *very* motivating and exciting because it works fast. Find this $100 per month by using the ideas we discussed earlier. Look for creative ways to cut spending.

While you're paying off your debts at an accelerated rate, be sure to still pay yourself 10% of your gross income each month. By saving *and* paying off your debt at the same time, you will experience great surges of internal power and excitement for life, which will create momentum to keep your plan going.

Many financial planners recommend that you have at least six months of savings for emergencies. If you've paid off your bills, you'll need less money and you will also have an enormous amount of cash flowing into your accounts. It would then only take a few months to save up enough to live on for a whole year.

So, in addition to paying yourself 10% first (money building fund), the next best thing you can do with your money is to pay off your debt. Paying off a 21% credit card is the same as investing into something that pays a 21% return! Debt-elimination is a great investment for your money—until it is paid off. Using this system will save you many years, and hundreds of thousands of dollars. You should be able to eliminate all debt within five to seven years, including your mortgage! Often, less time is required. Figure out how much of your paycheck you will be able to keep once you are totally debt-free. You will be abundantly wealthy, and be on an investment path to becoming financially independent. The next phase is to operate on 100% cash. If you want to make a purchase or take a trip, you will be able to pay cash for these items. Instead of using $5,000 to $20,000 in credit on a card, you'll have much more than this in cash. When you're living on a cash basis and are totally debt free, you'll be able to buy anything in your life that you want or need in just a few years. If you want to buy a new house, you will get a much better deal on it, if you pay cash for it. You will also have the opportunity to buy homes that have been discounted because of distress (divorces, deaths, tax sales or repossessions). You can purchase these homes at a considerable discount.

13. Never, never, never purchase anything on credit again. Very important—once you pay off all your debt, never, never, never purchase anything on credit again! I know that this sounds almost anti-American, but it is not! Living in debt is just the way we have been pro-grammed by the system. When you become debt-free and you are operating only on a cash basis, you will have a big chunk of money coming in every month that you were using towards all the bills that were financed. Since you are not used to actually living on this money, simply invest it into your money building fund to create more wealth for yourself. When you reach this point you will have an empowered attitude toward life and your finances. You may be pleasantly surprised to see how you have generated other avenues of income in your life.

Jose and Maria had been married for 14 years and had three lovely children. Although they had both worked for the same employer for 15 and 18 years respectively, they were impoverished. During our initial consultation session, I looked at their budget versus income. I found that they were not broke! Jose and Maria were simply mismanaging their money. They would frequently go out to eat and shop impulsively. Both of them justified their impulsive buying by saying that they worked hard for their money. After discovering a total combined income of $58,000, I explained to them that they were responsible for making their family live in a low-income town house in a very dangerous section of town. With reluctance, the two agreed to go on a budget and wealth producing system. They made it a family affair by involving the children in the money saving process by making it a fun challenge to see how much money could be saved to pay off bills and create their money building fund.

Nine months after meeting with Jose and Maria, they bought a beautiful home in a nice neighborhood. Their kids are able to play outside safely and go to great schools. Maria told me in a letter last month that she and Jose were studying stocks on a daily basis. They are beginning to make a decent profit on their initial stock investments, and they are anticipating paying off their home within two and a half years!

14. Take these two steps when you're debt-free and cash operative:

* Invest six months of expenses in a low risk vehicle, such as a money market fund or certificate of deposit. Open this account at your bank or through a stock broker.
* Establish a trust. There are many different types

of trusts that your attorney can tell you about. I use a living trust and make myself the trustee, which allows me to make decisions regarding the use of the proceeds from the trust. You will need to assign an additional trustee in the event of your death. Also, by having a trust, your estate won't be tied up in probate court upon your death.

Chapter 15 Review
Pay Off Your Debt

1. Realize lenders are not on your side. Anyone in the business of lending money is not working for you, even though they will try to make it look that way. This includes banks, lending institutions, and mortgage companies.

2. A home mortgage is not a good tax break. If you are in the 25% tax bracket, you will only get twenty-five cents back on your taxes for every dollar spent on your mortgage. Do not be fooled by this false tax break created by the lending institutions.

3. Any kind of credit gives a temporary false sense of wealth and security. You cannot reach financial independence by using consumer credit.

4. The worst credit drug of them all is the credit card. It's the opiate of the people.

5. Before you buy, ask yourself why. Most of the stress in our lives comes from participating in the credit system. When considering a purchase, stop and talk to yourself. Ask questions like, "Do I really need this right now? If so, why?"

6. You will find that as you accumulate money, you will want to buy less.

7. Overcome spending impulses.

8. The most crucial change that you can make is to operate completely on cash.

9. Accelerate your payments.

10. When paying bills off in an accelerated manner, make sure the lender knows that the additional money is intended for principal only. Otherwise it could be applied towards their interest. Mark additional payments "For principal only."

11. Use the magic of an accelerated "roll over" debt elimination system to get yourself completely out of debt fast.

12. Use the $100 key to freedom. Build a debt payoff account of at least $100 per month by eliminating impulse spending and trimming your budget.

13. Never purchase anything on credit again! Operate on one-hundred percent cash.

14. Take these two steps when you're debt-free and cash operative:

    * Invest six months' expenses in a low-risk vehicle.
    * Establish a trust.

CHAPTER 16

ATTITUDE

ATTITUDES ARE THE FORERUNNERS
OF CONDITIONS.

ERIC BUTTERWORTH

*

WHAT LIES BEHIND US AND WHAT
LIES BEFORE US ARE TINY MATTERS
COMPARED TO WHAT LIES WITHIN
US.

OLIVER WENDELL HOLMES

*

ATTITUDES ARE MORE IMPORTANT
THAN FACTS.

KARL A. MENNINGER

I t has been said that just as the set of the sail determines the direction of the boat, your *mindset* determines the direction of your life.

When I was researching the information for this book and doing consulting work, I found a number of people living what I would call a successful lifestyle, but their expensive cars, homes, vacations, and so on, were a result of living on credit cards which they were unable to pay off. As a result of our consultation together, they realized they were "renting" an elaborate lifestyle that could crumble at any moment. In many cases, it did. When they could no longer afford to rent their lifestyle, they were evicted from it!

It can be difficult to acquire the lifestyle of a Hollywood movie star, but it is even more difficult to maintain it! Most of us have been brainwashed by the media into believing that driving an expensive new car is much more pleasurable than driving a clean, dependable used car. Or, that living in a huge mansion is somehow much more enjoyable than living in a smaller, comfortable home. Most of us have come to believe that impressing the relatives and neighbors with our material possessions is more important than our peace of mind.

Sound familiar? Everybody wants a rich and famous lifestyle, right? What good is that scenario if it is a life of slavery to credit card bills? Any minute it could crumble, and often it does. The credit consumption mentality keeps you enslaved and constantly struggling. As you accumulate money, your mindset will change from getting out of debt to creating a true wealth consciousness. As you begin to change your attitude, and truly enjoy life and the accumulation of wealth, you will find that the desire to simplify your life increases.

A friend of mine, Deborah, lived among the celebrities in Beverly Hills, California. For years, she and her husband struggled to maintain a very affluent lifestyle: a mansion, cars, vacations, the country club life, celebrity parties, and so on. Outwardly they appeared rich and happy, but they literally owned nothing; even their clothes had been purchased on credit. Under the tremendous stress and financial pressure to maintain their lifestyle, the marriage slowly deteriorated into physical abuse and finally dissolved completely. Deborah has mentioned several times that struggling to maintain the *appearance* of wealth destroyed a marriage that was once beautiful.

Hear the wake-up call. It's a simple decision. If you want to change direction when you're sailing, simply change the set of the sail. It's the same in life. Change your mindset. It's crucial that you make the change *now*. Drop out of the fast-lane into a more balanced life. You will not only save an enormous amount of money, but you will actually increase the quality of your life as well.

Chapter 16 Review
Attitude

1. It has been said that just as the set of the sail determines the direction of the boat, your "mindset" determines the direction of your life. Examine your mindset.

2. It can be difficult to acquire the lifestyle of a Hollywood movie star, but it is even more difficult to maintain it! Most of us have been brainwashed by the media into believing we must live beyond our means.

3. As you accumulate money, your mindset will change from getting out of debt to creating true wealth.

4. Drop out of the fast-lane into a more balanced life. You will save money and actually increase the quality of your life.

CHAPTER 17

DEVELOPING PERSONAL POWER

FOR A PERSON TO BUILD A RICH AND REWARDING LIFE FOR HIMSELF, THERE ARE CERTAIN QUALITIES AND BITS OF KNOWLEDGE HE NEEDS TO ACQUIRE. THERE ARE ALSO HARMFUL ATTITUDES, SUPERSTITIONS, AND EMOTIONS THAT HE NEEDS TO CHIP AWAY.

A PERSON NEEDS TO CHIP AWAY AT EVERYTHING THAT DOESN'T LOOK LIKE THE PERSON HE OR SHE MOST WANTS TO BECOME.

EARL NIGHTINGALE

TRY NOT! DO, OR DO NOT. THERE IS NO TRY.

YODA

I frequently speak to groups of people about money—how to make it, keep it, and live debt free. Although money is an important facet in life, there are other aspects of life that are critical to success.

Here are some of the secrets of personal power:

P— Power hour. Spend the first part of your day, planning, previewing and praying.

I believe in a superior energy called God. It is this supreme energy and belief that is responsible for countless miracles in my life. In addition to praying, I write in a journal everyday. I keep track of what is going on in my life. I journal what I accomplished the day before, and the goals for the present day (which I put in the form of a "things to do list.") Simply listing your daily goals in written form in the morning can actually double or triple your productivity for the day.

As I pass into the next world, I plan to leave my journals behind for others to see the inner workings of my thinking. Besides leaving this legacy, a journal is an automatic feedback system. It cues me up on a daily basis and lets me know if I am achieving my mark—my personal best. A journal can also be an extremely powerful therapeutic tool.

O— Others. Remember other people.

Near death experiences have allowed us a glimpse at what happens when people have died and come back. The common message that all people have returned with is that the general purpose of life is simply to learn and to love. By learning and loving you will be fulfilling the master plan for your life.

W— Work. Work is fun.

Since humans are only happy when they are producing, develop the attitude that you enjoy your work. Many people have said to me, "Be careful or you'll burn out." I always smile and say, "I'd rather burn out than rust out." (Neil Young said it first.) Always do the hardest and scariest job first. When you confront and accomplish the "worst first," you develop a sense of high self-esteem because you realize that you can do anything.

E— Exercise. You must do some kind of physical activity every day.

Research indicates that exercising for even five minutes a day can make a significant difference in the quality of your health. So just commit to five minutes of exercise daily.

An old Arabic formula for wealth goes like this: When thinking of one million dollars, the number "one" represents your health. The zeros behind that number represent your job, family, friends, house, car, jewels, and so on. If you take away the "one," what are you left with? A bunch of zeros. Do not be foolish by ignoring your body.

R— Review. Go over your accomplishments at the end of each day. Take an hour at the end of your week, a day at the end of the month, and a weekend at the end of the year for review.

Analyze what you want, and see if you have taken the steps to make it happen. Never be afraid to correct your course whenever necessary. Real personal power or success that is whole and satisfying is not solely the result of stockpiling incredible amounts of money! In addition to the appearance of what most of us would call "success," you must cultivate a finer quality of inner life in order to be at peace, and to fully enjoy life. Some people believe that you cannot be a nice person and have lots of power and money. I challenge that belief! Becoming a truly powerful person goes beyond having power and money. *Who you become* in the process of acquiring power and money is actually more important than the power and money itself.

I challenge you to take a journey with me. Let us be determined to develop beliefs and habits that will allow the achievement of great wealth—and in the process become gracious, passionate and strong human beings. Are you up for this challenge? It is an *exciting* journey!

Treating each person with compassion, dignity and respect begins first with treating yourself that way, and then knowing you are worthy of receiving the same from others. You must also hold yourself accountable to a higher, more loving power greater than yourself. So, in the context of our journey to power and success, when a reference is made to "success", the definition automatically includes developing a rich inner self that outwardly expresses the qualities of compassion, wisdom and strength, as well as other virtues.

The path to becoming truly powerful is an exciting roller-coaster ride of self-discovery. On this ride, you will need a strong curiosity about life combined with self-discipline, intuition and creativity. These qualities can be developed, so don't worry if you think you do not have enough of these qualities right now. Just take these ideas into your heart and mind, and you will be surprised at how easily and quickly these qualities will become consistent internal habits. Once you begin the process of implementing the suggestions for wealth and character building, you will be so energized that your life will change dramatically. As you become more powerful, you must be willing to develop these higher internal qualities in greater degrees, and then combine them with the "action" of serving others. When you travel the path of becoming this kind of success, power and money will automatically be attracted to you as a result of your new attitudes and actions. Even if you have tried and failed many times, I want you to know that you can change your life starting today.

There is a special power inside each of us. This power is housed in our brain. We only use 1/1,000,000 of our brain. The best exercise for the brain is reading. Read everything you can on the subjects that interest you. Make a habit of reading thirty to sixty minutes a day. This works out to approximately two books a month.

You will be amazed at how much your life will change just by doing this one thing. Keep reading material by your bed and read for fifteen minutes before turning out the light. And even in the bathroom—you would be amazed how much reading you can get done in there! Keep a book in your car in case you get stuck in traffic or find yourself waiting for some other reason. Every moment in your life is precious. Do not waste any time.

Your brain, or your conscious mind, controls the subconscious part of your mind in either a negative or a positive way. When you engage in thinking, you are engaging your conscious mind. The subconscious part of your mind is the same energy as God. This dynamic energy works within us, creating and bringing form into the material world. The only way you can talk to the subconscious part of your mind is with your conscious mind. It works like this:

Whatever you tell yourself goes from your conscious mind into your subconscious mind.

What happens next in your life is the result of the *degree of conviction you felt* when you gave yourself the message. Listen to the difference in these two statements, and ask yourself which one sounds more convincing: "I am a powerful person?" (timid and meek) Or, "I am a powerful person!" (with power and conviction). If you send a message to the subconscious mind that you are "trying" to create wealth, then that is exactly what you will be doing. You will always find yourself in circumstances where you are "trying." You will never actually achieve it! Be careful what you ask for—the subconscious mind creates only according to desire plus conviction. So, don't "try" anything, make a decision to "do" it, and stick with it.

For one day, think only positive thoughts. If something negative comes up, immediately replace that thought with a statement of faith. Say, "I have faith that all is well with this." Then take immediate action on something you can change about that particular issue, or take action on something else in your life. If you forget and fall back into the old pattern of complaining or negative thinking, do not waste time beating yourself up. Remember *like attracts like!* Simply notice what you did, and recommit with determination and conviction to your new plan of faith and action. After one day, extend your commitment to the next day and the next, and so on. You will be amazed at how this will change every aspect of your life. Your subconscious mind and the great power of the universe will begin lining up all the good things you are imagining for yourself. That is how we co-create with God. The real reason it might take a long time to receive the good things we dream about is the amount and consistency of our own convictions. The more confidence you have in achieving your dreams, the faster they come into your life.

The next ingredient in creating personal power is attitude. Some may say, "attitude, shmattitude—so what?" Historically, if you were to examine the lives of the people behind the majority of significant discoveries or social movements, you will find at least one characteristic that they had in common: They all had a positive and persistent attitude about themselves and their intentions. Attitude is powerful, and it's the most important element in achieving success.

This incredible universal power is available to everyone everywhere! Actually, your attitude is already directing this power. Whatever circumstances you are experiencing in your life right now, your attitude has directed it to create. Are you satisfied with what you have created? All it takes for you to change is to realize the power you are throwing away by settling for the status quo. You have the power to create anything you want in life! If you are tired of feeling bored, why not make the decision to change something in your life today? Free yourself from the prison of mediocrity and live a life of passion. The two questions you must answer in life are, "Who do I want to become?" and, "What do I want to create?" Decide to use the power of your attitude to benefit yourself and others.

There was an experiment conducted which demonstrated a phenomenon called, "Learned Helplessness." A healthy dog was placed in a wire cage divided in half by a partition. The partition was low enough that the dog could jump from one side to the other. Each side of the cage floor was wired with a separate electric grid controlled by switches that enabled the experimenters to turn the electricity up, down, or off. When the dog was placed in the cage, he jumped over the partition to the "cold" side when the current was turned on. The experiment was repeated many times and the dog learned to jump off the "hot" side at the first sign of the current. When the experimenters turned the electricity on in both sides on at the same time, the dog jumped from side to side, and then finally lay down and took the heat. The dog had learned that no matter what it did, it could not escape.

At one time or another in your life, you might have felt like that dog. We have all been there, and some of you may believe that that's just the way life is. But that's not how the experiment ended. After the dog gave up and lay on the hot floor, the experimenters opened the door of the cage to allow it to escape. To their utter amazement the dog refused to come out even though it was in pain! *You are much smarter than that poor dog!* Don't let your fear keep you in the cage! Take charge of your life and your destiny! Change your attitude! Use the incredible universal power inside you to set goals, take action and achieve your dreams!

Many of us are simply punishing ourselves by two serious disease processes referred to as "stinking thinking" and "hardening of the attitude." Stinking thinking is choosing to think about the negative side of life and talking about the negative side of others. Hardening of the attitude is when you refuse to change your negative traits. Both of these disease processes are serious because they rob you of life! Many people choose drugs, drinking alcohol, overeating, and so on, to escape these diseases. I am always amazed when people say, "Let's get high and have a drink or smoke a joint." These things do not get you high, they actually depress you and shut you down. If you want more excitement or more of a high, then you need to enjoy the energy of life. You cannot enjoy the energy of life when you are down or spaced out on drugs and alcohol.

Just for a minute, close your eyes, take a deep breath and exhale slowly. Imagine the person that you want to become in the future. How do you look, act, dress, think, and feel? Without judgment, think about the person you are today. What differences do you see? Write them down. Explain how you would become the person you just imagined. What steps would you take to become that person? Bridging the gap between who you are now and who you intend to become depends on recognizing and using your own internal power and strength. But first, you must change your attitude towards yourself and life in general. Write down and answer these four questions on a separate piece of paper:

* How do I feel about myself right now? What do I like? What don't I like?
* How do I feel about life right now? What do I like about my life, and what don't I like about my life?
* What do I believe about myself right now? Answer the question, "I am...." as many times as you can.
* What do I believe about life right now? Answer the question, "Life is...." until you explain your view fully.

After you have written down your answers to the questions above, imagine again the person that you want to become. Close your eyes and get a clear picture or feeling about who you want to become. What would that person believe about him or herself? What would that person believe about life? Complete the same questions again and write those answers down.

If you have taken the time to really think about and answer these questions, you are very close to bridging the gap. The only thing lacking are the action steps necessary to make it come true for you. Self-image is based on beliefs learned from positive and negative life experiences. If you believe you are good at something, you will attract experiences which confirm that belief. If you believe you are bad at something, you will attract experiences which confirm that belief. Life is a mirror. You get back the energy and thoughts you put out. The fastest way to increase your personal power and acquire wealth is to change what you think about yourself and money!

Although she had been working for thirty years, Joan had never made over $21,000 in a year. When I sat down with her, she said, "I love money, but I don't want to learn about stocks, finance, taxes, real estate, or any of that boring stuff." I told her that was fine and started packing my briefcase. She wanted to know why I was preparing to leave and I told her that I could not help her if she was not willing to put forth any effort to learn about the subject. Joan asked me to stay and said, "I do need to make a change in my life. I'm tired of living from paycheck to paycheck." In one month , Joan was talking to me about the stock market as if she had been investing for years. One day while we were talking on the phone, she caught herself in mid-sentence and said, "I can't believe that this finance stuff is so interesting!" Today, Joan makes more in one month than she did in an entire year.

Chapter 17 Review
Developing Personal Power

1. Although money is one facet of your life, there are very important inner aspects of your life critical to your success.

2. Using the word "POWER" as an acronym, follow these five disciplines and be surprised:

    P—Power hour. Use the first part of your day for planning, previewing and prayer.

    O—Others. Remember other people. By learning and loving you will be fulfilling the master plan for your life.

    W—Work. Work is fun.

    E—Exercise. You must be physically active every day. Even five minutes is beneficial.

    R—Review. Go over your accomplishments at the end of each day; for an hour at the end of your week; a day at the end of the month; a weekend at the end of the year.

3. As you become powerful, you must be willing to develop these higher internal qualities and combine them with the "action" of serving others.

4. There is a special power inside each one of us—in the brain. The best exercise for the brain is reading, which allows us to access more of that power.

5. Your brain, or your conscious mind, controls the subconscious part of your mind in either a negative or a positive way.

6. Don't *try*. Make the decision to *do* it. Then stick with it.

7. For one day, think only positive thoughts. If something negative comes up, *immediately* replace that thought with a statement of faith. Tell yourself, "I have faith that all is well with this." This is part of developing mental discipline.

8. Remember the "Learned Helplessness," experiment with the dog in the cage. You are much smarter than a dog. Make a plan and take action.

9. Avoid abuse of drugs and alcohol. Remember, moderation is the key to mastering life.

10. Bridging the gap between who you are now and who you intend to become depends on recognizing your own internal power and strength. Recognizing your internal power and strength depends totally on changing your attitude towards yourself and life in general. Take the time to answer the questions in the exercise. You're worth it!

11. Self-image is based on beliefs learned from positive and negative life experiences. You will be attracted to, or avoid situations depending on what you believe about yourself.

The good news is that no matter what your experiences have been in the past, you can change your beliefs!

CHAPTER 18

FEAR

HE WHO IS AFRAID OF A THING
GIVES IT POWER OVER HIM.

MOORISH PROVERB

*

WE ARE GIVEN ONE LIFE, AND THE
DECISION IS OURS WHETHER TO
WAIT FOR CIRCUMSTANCES TO
MAKE UP OUR MIND OR WHETHER
TO ACT, AND IN ACTING, LIVE.

OMAR NELSON BRADLEY

*

THOUGH A RIGHTEOUS
MAN FALLS SEVEN TIMES,
HE RISES AGAIN.

PROVERBS 24:16

The main emotion that prevents people from being more positive is fear. Fear is a barrier that locks you into a prison made of your own imagination. Fear turns you against yourself. You can and must change thoughts of fear into habitual powerful, positive thoughts.

Think of the word FEAR as an acronym for False Evidence About Reality. Fear is not real. It is an emotion that *we* create about the *future*. You can only be fearful when you are inactive or contemplating something that is about to happen. The fastest way to cure fear is to take action. When you are faced with a future fearful situation, take whatever action you can to resolve it. As soon as you go into action, you will lose your fear. You can't be afraid of something while going into action to resolve it. If there's no physical action that you can take, you must use mental discipline to refrain from judging the outcome by having faith that the infinite power of the universe works all things together for good.

Let's say you and a group of friends want to go skydiving. You would first decide to attend classes. During the classes your fear would most likely surface as you watch videos, study what to do and not do, practice wearing your parachute and landing properly. Finally, the day comes for your first jump. Everyone tensely chatters while driving to the plane. As you climb into the plane, your stomach is in knots, and your fear multiplies each second you ascend into the air. You can feel your heart thumping in your throat, and you are probably thinking, along with everyone else, "Why did I ever decide to do this crazy thing!" When the door flies open, you are convinced your life is over! Suddenly it is your turn to jump! Out you fall! Amazingly, as soon as you jump out, your fear vanishes! Why? Because you are *in action!* You clearly recall what you need to do and calmly concentrate on it. And you are even surprised by thrilling moments of pure joy and wild exhilaration! That is exactly how life can and should be for all of us! Fear can *only* exist when you are inactive. Eliminate your fears right now by taking action toward resolving the *assumed* (and therefore false) outcomes. You will automatically become a more peaceful and powerful person.

Brian never would have guessed fear was blocking his prosperity. After working for over eight years on the same job, Brian had saved approximately $32,000. When I started working with him, I noticed how he would get physically agitated when I talked about investing his $32,000. His pupils would dilate and his face would go white whenever I mentioned putting some of his savings into high risk stocks. I asked Brian why he was afraid? He said, "I can't stand the thought of losing everything that I've saved for the past eight years." I totally understood, and agreed with him. The thought of losing everything was scary. I recommended that he go into action by starting with a portion of his savings and then work from there.

After studying the subject of investing, Brian took $16,000 and invested it into small cap stocks. Within six months his $16,000 had grown to over $32,000. A year later Brian's investment had grown to over $100,000. When I asked Brian what he thought was his biggest reason for doing so well with his investments, he replied, "You taught me to overcome my fears by going into action. Once I went into action, I was too busy learning and investing to worry about losing my initial investment. I was more concerned with making it grow." When you invest in the stock market or any other investment vehicle, you might not do as well as Brian, but you can't do anything if you let fear hold you back from taking action. You can't effectively drive forward in your car while applying the brakes! When addressing the subject of taking consistent action, Abraham Lincoln said: "I may be a slow walker, but I never walk backwards." Stay in the forward action mode.

Chapter 18 Review
Fear

1. The main emotion that prevents people from being more positive is fear. Fear is a barrier that locks you into a prison made of your own imagination. It turns you against yourself.

2. One acronym for fear is False Evidence About Reality.

3. You can only experience fear when you are *inactive* and *assume* you already know the outcome of a future event. Stay out of judgement. Proceed with faith!

4. The fastest way to cure fear is to take action. When you are faced with a fearful situation in the present or future, get into action to resolve it. As soon as you go into action to resolve the problem, you will lose your fear.

CHAPTER 19

BALANCING
YOUR LIFE

I HEAR AND I FORGET,
I SEE AND I REMEMBER,
I DO AND I UNDERSTAND.

CHINESE PROVERB

*

FAITH IS THE HIGHEST PASSION IN
A HUMAN BEING. MANY IN EVERY
GENERATION MAY NOT COME THAT
FAR, BUT NONE COMES FURTHER.

SOREN KIERKEGAARD

*

PERFECTION IS FOUND IN
THE SINCERE ATTEMPT AT
BALANCE IN LIFE.

Q. SOLOMON

A happy life is a balanced life. A balanced, happy life is a powerful life. Regardless of monetary achievements, a successful person is one who is able to maintain balance in life. Notice how you participate in life. Don't be so rushed and unbalanced that you overlook the important things. Concentrate on balancing these six areas of life:

1. Self

Are you truly taking care of your body? Are you abusing any portion of it? Are you scheduling consistent and periodic time for quiet reflection and relaxation to refresh both your mind and body? Are you watching your diet? Are you doing at least five minutes of exercise per day?

2. Family and Relationships

Are you truly serving your family? Relationships are not about what we are getting out of them, but what we are *bringing to* them. If you're having a marriage problem, then you must concentrate on what you can contribute to make the marriage or relationship better. If you're having problems with a spouse or child, try to see the world through their eyes.

3. Work

Are you truly giving everything you can to your present business or employer? If someone tells me they are unhappy with their current job, I always ask, "Why are you still there?" The usual reply is money. That is not a good reason. As a matter of fact, if you are receiving money from a job that you do not like, and you are not giving 100% of yourself for the money you do receive, then in a sense you are stealing.

Many people say, "I don't know exactly what I want to do with my life." Do the purpose finder exercise in this book. Try different things, but don't waste your life sitting in indecision.

4. The Human Race

People usually think, "What can one person do to help the human race?" That is up to you to find out. It is the responsibility of everyone on this planet to contribute something back into the family of humanity. History overflows with stories of ordinary individuals like you and me who have influenced the quality of life for everyone worldwide throughout time.

5. Our Planet and the Animal Kingdom

Are you doing your part to improve our planet in some way? Are you helping to protect the animals? Remember, they were here first and since we are the superior beings, it is our responsibility to take care of them and this beautiful place we call home.

6. God/Spirit/Soul

Are you taking care of the spirit by prayer or daily meditation? Are you studying to expand your consciousness? Are you taking spiritual seminars? Ask yourself, "Am I demonstrating that I trust God (faith)?" The best way to love God is by demonstrating your trust that all is well no matter what, and giving thanks for the abundance that you already have. No matter how much or how little you have, give thanks for the abundance that is yours now!

These six areas are not in prioritized order. They're all equal in importance. As you strive for balance you will earn the respect of others. More importantly, you will respect yourself. It may not be possible to balance all six areas of your life at all times. Try to balance as many of them as you can regularly. Just by attempting to balance the six areas, you will be happier, and bring more happiness to those around you.

Another ingredient of personal power is *passion for life.* The fundamental secret to becoming powerful and wealthy is to be passionate about what you are doing! Don't make money your primary motivation. A very wealthy friend of mine once told me that if I did the right things long enough, I would be successful, but more importantly, I would be happy. Jim Rohn, a very successful businessman and motivational speaker describes success as "a few simple disciplines practiced every day."

Discover your passions, then increase your skills in those areas and find a way to share them with others every day. Jim Rohn also says, "Never ask yourself, 'What am I getting from this job or this relationship?' The real question is, 'What am I *becoming* in this job or this relationship?'" Take a few minutes right now to explore what kind of person you are becoming. If you are unhappy with what you find, make the internal changes necessary to create happiness. Use the techniques presented in this book.

An interesting way to discover what you are passionate about is to imagine what you would do if you won ten million dollars in the lottery. How would you spend your time if you did not need the money? Ask yourself, "If money were no object, and I had all the confidence in the world, what would I do?" Your answer will help reveal what you truly desire for your life. Do it now. Write it down.

More money may make your life more physically comfortable, but it is not going to automatically make you feel truly fulfilled and happy. You must have a bigger purpose. Earn your money by doing something that fulfills you along the way. This will ensure that you will be able to maintain *both* your money *and* your happiness over time.

As you master the fundamentals contained in this book, you will find yourself automatically choosing areas of expertise that you are passionate about. For example, suppose you have a passion to study weight loss. There are thousands of diet books on the market. They all address three main areas: right attitude, right nutrition, and right exercise. The more you focus on these three fundamentals, the more knowledge and experience you will gain and the more conviction you will feel. With conviction, you will master it easily.

I always ask people to tell me what they like to do during their time off. This helps me discover what kind of a person they are on the inside. For instance, if someone excessively drinks alcohol during time off, they are probably an alcoholic on the inside. But if you asked them, they would probably reply that they are just trying to relax a little. There is an old saying, "Actions speak louder than words." What are your actions saying to others around you? What are your actions saying to yourself? Are you listening? Treat yourself to your own "quality time" on your time off. Do what you truly love to do and don't try to escape. Life is too precious to waste!

Olivia was a hard working mother of three. She worked as a hairdresser ten hours a day, six days a week. When she would get off work at night, she would race home, rush in and say hello to the children. Then she would sit down, turn on the television, and drink a few beers. Olivia justified this routine by saying that she worked hard as a single parent and deserved the "pleasure" of unwinding at the end of the day. She was amazed when her fourteen year old daughter was picked up at a local park one night for drinking! When Olivia went to get her daughter at the police station, her daughter said she was just trying to relax and have some fun. She felt that since she worked hard at school all day, and then came home to help with the house and the other kids, that she deserved to have a little "pleasure" after working hard all day. Sound familiar?

Parents teach their children by their actions, not by their words. Olivia accepted her wake-up call! She stopped her nightly drinking and became more involved with her children during the evening. Olivia's daughter has graduated from college and is now a therapist specializing in drug and alcohol rehabilitation. Olivia is relieved, empowered by her decision, and much happier with her own life!

Chapter 19 Review
Balancing Your Life

1.   A happy life is a balanced life. A balanced, happy life is a powerful life. Regardless of monetary achievements, a successful person is one who is able to keep all areas in their life balanced.

2.   Pace yourself by concentrating on balancing these six areas of life:

> *Self*—Are you truly taking care of your body? Are you abusing any portion of your body? Are you taking periodic and consistent breaks to refresh both your mind and body? Are you watching your diet? Are you doing at least five minutes of exercise per day?

> *Family/Personal Relationships*—Are you truly serving your family? Relationships are not about what we are getting out of them, but what we are *bringing to* them.

> *Work*—Are you truly giving everything you have to give to your present business or employer?

> *The Human Race*—People often ask, "What can one person do to help the human race?" That is up to you to find out. It is your responsibility to contribute back into the family of humans on this planet. History overflows with stories of average individuals who have made wonderful changes. Why not be one of them?

> *Our Planet and the Animal Kingdom*—Are you doing your part to improve this planet in

some way? Are you taking care of the animals?

God/Spirit/Soul—Take care of the spirit by praying or meditating daily. Expand your consciousness.

3.   Another ingredient for personal power is *passion* for life. The fundamental secret to becoming powerful and wealthy is this: Be passionate about what you are doing! Don't make money your primary motivation. Have a deeper, passionate purpose. Use money to support it.

4.   As you master the fundamentals in this book, you will begin to know yourself deeply, and as a result, you will automatically start choosing areas of expertise you're passionate about.

CHAPTER 20

TIME MANAGEMENT

IF AT FIRST YOU DON'T SUCCEED,
DELEGATE !

UNKNOWN

*

PASSION FOR MY WORK SENDS
ME RUNNING TO MY DESK EVERY
MORNING. AND MY TO DO LIST
GIVES ME THE FREEDOM TO
LEAVE MY DESK AT NIGHT.

L. J. MARKHAM

*

SOMEBODY SHOULD TELL US
RIGHT AT THE START OF OUR
LIVES THAT WE ARE DYING. THEN
WE MIGHT LIVE LIFE TO THE
LIMIT, EVERY MINUTE OF EVERY
DAY. *DO IT!* I SAY. WHATEVER YOU
WANT TO DO, DO IT <u>NOW</u>! THERE
ARE ONLY SO MANY TOMORROWS.

MICHAEL LANDON

Time management can be reduced to one basic idea: *Learn to delegate.* The Pareto Principle states that 80% of our results are achieved by 20% of our actions. That means 80% of your activity is wasted! Unsuccessful people get stuck in the 80%, and then delay doing the crucial 20% by procrastinating! Successful people do the opposite. They figure out the 20% of their actions that make them successful, master those, and then delegate the other 80%. Figure out the things that you are passionate about. Then realize that because you feel passionate about them, you probably have a God-given talent in those areas. This is your inner-self revealing your purpose to you. As humans we measure our lives using time. In light of this, how we manage our time indicates how we appreciate our lives. You won't be an effective time manager or value your time if what you are doing with your time is not connected in some way to your passion or deeper purpose. The average person has approximately 630,720 hours in their lifetime. The importance of these hours aren't usually appreciated until the last few are upon us.

The tools we use to help us manage time are clocks, calendars, goals, action steps and "surging." Clocks and watches keep track of parts of the day. The calendar orients us to the months of the year. Goals help us keep track of where we are going with our lives, giving us direction as well as helping us evaluate our progress. Action steps control our goals, and determine the level of wealth, intelligence, prosperity, and even love that we have in our lives. By creating deadlines (goals with dates) and taking action steps, we can make our dreams come true. Surging makes goals happen *now* as you give undivided attention for a specific period of time to a certain project or part of a project.

I know a lady who cleans her house using the principle of surging. She sets a timer in each room as she cleans, and usually beats the time frame she gives herself. As a result, she has more time to do the things she really enjoys.

Time is not real. It was created by human beings.We use it to keep track of our lives, but it doesn't really exist. You can break through the falsehood of time by getting more things done and enjoying life to its fullest potential.

After interviewing many people in their last days of life, I was amazed to discover that most of them would have lived their lives differently! I decided not to let that happen to me. I learned at a young age that we must live everyday as if it were our last, but plan as if we will live forever. With this philosophy you cannot fail. You will be accomplishing everything you want to do and truly live a happy life. Success and acquiring personal power are mainly mental and spiritual disciplines. It is through the power of our minds, and living a life of compassion, strength and goodness that we are able to achieve anything!

One of the most important things you can do to manage your time is to operate from a daily Things To Do list. When you write all your goals down on a daily basis, you won't forget anything; your production will improve by 75%. Regardless of your lifestyle, use a Things To Do list and you will live a more effective and productive life.

Chapter 20 Review
Time Management

1. Time management in a nutshell: *Learn to delegate.*

2. Remember the Pareto Principle: 80% of our results are achieved by 20% of our actions. Figure out the 20% and do those.

3. Operate from a daily Things To Do list. Regardless of your lifestyle, use a daily Things To Do list and live a more time-effective and productive life.

CHAPTER 21

THE SECRET
BENEFITS OF A
HOME BUSINESS

GOODWILL IS THE ONE
AND ONLY ASSET THAT
COMPETITION CANNOT
UNDERSELL OR DESTROY.

MARSHALL FIELD

*

IF YOU DON'T LIKE SWIMMING WITH
THE SHARKS, OPEN A BAIT SHOP.

UNKNOWN

*

BUSINESS HAS ONLY TWO
FUNCTIONS—MARKETING AND
INNOVATION.

PETER F. DRUCKER

Y ou can make more money right out of your home than you ever dreamed possible. I have never met anyone who became wealthy working for someone else. If you want to accumulate wealth, you will have to start your own business. It does not have to be a big business. The fastest growing sect of businesses in America is the home business. In 1994, there were approximately five million home businesses. In 1995, that number grew to over nine million. By the year 2000, it is estimated that there will be almost twenty million home businesses in this country.

America is based on the premise of free enterprise. Living in America means that if you have an idea and the willingness to make that idea come to life, then you can go into business for yourself. If you are willing to apply yourself in your business, you have the opportunity to become wealthy. Marketing is the key to business success. Make sure you read books on marketing your business or product. Step-by-step guides can be purchased from a bookstore, or borrowed from your public library on such topics as how to start, finance, market and manage your own business.

There are many techniques you can use to discover ideas for your product, service or business. One of the best ways to find a business idea is to sit down with some close friends or family members and brainstorm. Besides being a lot of fun, you will be surprised at the wealth of ideas you get

There are two important guidelines to help you start your own ideal business:

1. Operate from your home. This will give you great tax advantages and flexibility in your schedule and lifestyle. Take a tax course or research the requirements necessary for tax benefits.

2. Handle information. This is the Information Age. Everyone wants to discover ways to relay information more quickly and easily. Your information must be important and easy to use. If you have a good idea, some expertise and a powerful marketing plan you can become a millionaire.

To discover the ideal product or service for your business, use these four ideas :

* Identify a core human desire or need.
* Find a new technology for solving this desire or need.
* Find a new way to market this core desire or need.
* Teach individuals and groups what you have learned. Write a book based on your experiences and sell it.

Everything you have experienced in your life has value. Look at your successes and failures, and then let everyone else look at them too. I believe each of us is a walking history book. Put your story on paper and turn your life experiences into money. Even if you mistakenly believe you are a failure, people would be interested in your story.

Regardless of the business you decide to start, marketing is going to be a key factor in your success or failure. You can combine a great product with a poor marketing campaign and end up with a failed business. But you can combine an average or mediocre product and a great marketing campaign and be very successful.

Here are several ways to market your business:

* Classified, display and full-page ads.
* Television commercials or infomercials.
* Word-of-mouth or telling others directly.

In the information business, you have an unlimited, worldwide market. You can research these markets, create your product, test it and then begin production.

Three skills needed for your business are:

1. Learn how to research and create your product.
When you get one good idea, become the expert in your field. People will gravitate toward the expert. You must be among the top ten. Ask yourself, "What is it that others need or want to know?" It does not take years to become an expert. You can also find an expert who is under-marketed and bring their ideas to the market-place.

2. Learn how to package your product. If you have a great idea but poor packaging, you lose. After you find the best prices for your product materials, you must create a useful, eye-catching, low cost package.

3. Learn how to market your product. Marketing is essential! If you have excellent marketing, you can sell anything. Books are one of the best places to learn marketing skills. Here are five core marketing skills:

* Learn where to discover hoards of hungry buyers.
* Write compelling copy.
* Understand the psychology of human nature.
* Learn the secrets of direct mail advertisement.
* Learn how to track results and manage a data base.

Don't attempt to go into business without first identifying your life's purpose. This should be something that you are passionate about. A business without purpose will have no chance of survival. Once you have chosen the type of product or service you want for your business, define your market by looking for groups of people or businesses that are:

* Easily identified, large and growing;
* Hungry—having an immediate need, desire, or problem they are highly motivated to solve;
* Able and willing to buy.

Think of your market as a school of fish. Does it contain enough fish? Is your population growing or declining? Are they easy to find? What is their feeding pattern? Are they really hungry, or pretty much satisfied? What environment has ideal fishing conditions? Is there a certain food that makes them bite like crazy?

After you have defined your market, there are five important ingredients in your success:

1. Become an expert. Succeed in your core area of expertise by creating a new technology or by using an existing technology with a new marketing strategy. If you are not sure what area to focus on, go back to your purpose finder exercise. Research the ideas around which you based your purpose. If you find that some of the ideas have already been done, don't be discouraged. All you need is a solid product or service, a great title, an eye-catching package, and a superior marketing campaign, and a sincere desire to help others. With those five strategies alone you can leap over anyone who has come before you. Once you have identified your market and the best ways to get your information to your market, you are ready to take action.

Do not try to please everybody. Instead, please yourself. By doing this, you will reach everyone because you will be focused and clear. In other words, use your passion to find your niche.

2. Teach others. Give others the opportunity to learn the knowledge that you have acquired along the way to becoming an expert. You must accomplish your basic goals in the niche you have chosen *before* you begin teaching, so you can command the respect that an expert deserves. Then teach others to succeed as well.

3. Explore related fields. Discover other areas of information that relate to your area of expertise, and figure out how you use it to help others. For example, if you are also a successful salesperson, you might want to teach other sales people your techniques.

4. Use database marketing. A database is simply the names, addresses, telephone numbers and occupations of the people you have met. It's extremely important to select products carefully in order to maintain a high level of trust with the individuals on your data base. Approach them by doing the following:

* Selectively rent your list to other businesses. Other businesses will be willing to pay you money to rent your database. Be sure you use good judgment in choosing whom to rent your list to, so that you protect the integrity of your list.
* Generate leads for other businesses by giving a hearty endorsement of someone else's product to your database.
* Create a joint venture partnership, and split the profits on the products sold to your database.
* Become a direct marketer to your own database after carefully choosing your products.

*   Provide support services to businesses by becoming a copywriter, printer, mailing list printer, venture capitalist, business coach, public relations consultant, and so on.

5. *Create a seminar circuit.* Your ideas can reach hundreds of people, and possibly change or even save their lives. Start with two or more people and work up to more. You'll be able to create a base of interest, and as a result, offer individual consultations, and perhaps periodic coaching to the participants who want more in-depth information.

How do you attract loyal customers? The best and simplest way I've found is to run newspaper ads for free seminars or lectures. If it sounds simple, that's because it is. The people who attend your seminars can be automatically considered warm leads. They are normally very receptive to the information you will be presenting. You can usually count on 10% of the participants purchasing whatever you are promoting, either another seminar or products or both. Over time, every customer in your database can channel thousands of dollars into your business, just by offering them an exceptional service and value for their money. Sometimes it is a very wise decision to spend a little money up front on ads or free offers to ensure building a strong, long-term customer base. Most people are bombarded by hoards of marketing from competitors. You must take care of your customers. This will keep them loyal and focused on the great benefit they receive from doing business with you instead of your competitors. If possible, send cards for birthdays, holidays and anniversaries. If you spend one percent of your profits on cultivating your inner circle, you will profit thousands. Spend pennies to make dollars.

Chapter 21 Review
The Secret Benefits of a Home Business

1. If you want to have wealth, you must start your own business.

2. To come up with a business idea, sit down with family members or close friends and brainstorm without judgment.

3. If you can operate your business from your home, you can take advantage of tax breaks.

4. The ideal business involves using information as a product or service.

5. Marketing is the key factor in determining the success or failure of a business.

6. Explore related fields.

7. Create a data base.

8. Create a seminar circuit. Teach others what you have learned.

CHAPTER 22

CASHING IN ON THOSE IDEAS IN YOUR HEAD

WHAT IS OPPORTUNITY, AND WHEN
DOES IT KNOCK? IT NEVER KNOCKS!
YOU CAN WAIT A WHOLE LIFETIME,
LISTENING, HOPING, AND YOU WILL
HEAR NO KNOCKING. NONE AT ALL.
YOU ARE YOUR OPPORTUNITY, AND
YOU MUST KNOCK ON THE DOOR
LEADING TO YOUR DESTINY. YOU
PREPARE YOURSELF TO RECOGNIZE
OPPORTUNITY, TO PURSUE AND
SEIZE IT AS YOU DEVELOP THE
STRENGTH OF YOUR PERSONALITY,
AND BUILD A SELF-IMAGE WITH
WHICH YOU ARE ABLE TO LIVE, WITH
YOUR SELF-RESPECT ALIVE AND
GROWING.

MAXWELL MALTZ

How many times have you told yourself, "Hey, I can improve on that!" or said, "I thought of that three years ago, and there it is!" and then got mad at yourself for not taking action on your ideas? Here are 12 action steps you can take that will turn those ideas in your head into cash:

1. Identify or create a mailing list (database). When you meet people, ask for their business cards or write down their names, addresses, telephone numbers and occupations. This will become your data base. Another way to create a data base is to consult with one of the many mailing list brokers who advertise in a direct marketing magazine. Or a marketing consultant can help to identify a current list of potential customers who might be interested in your information. These sources can be found under Direct Mailers in the yellow pages. The characteristics to look for in a list should follow the guidelines mentioned earlier, such as a large and growing audience that is hungry and ready for a feeding frenzy.

Constantly build your data base. This means you need to make a habit of collecting people's names, addresses and telephone numbers. Important people you should add to your mailing list are friends, associates, co-workers, and anyone else that you meet during the rest of your life. Be sincere about wanting to help them improve their lives using products you believe in! You must also develop a profile of your ideal customer.

Describe in detail your target audience. What are their demographics, such as age, where they live, annual income range, interests, the magazines they read, and so on. Your local librarian can help you locate this information, and also the products that people want and need. It will also keep you from investing in a product or service that no one will buy.

Also include in your survey a question to find out what companies your customers are already using. The survey should contain questions that are easy to answer and it should not take more than five minutes for the individual to complete verbally or in writing.

3. Determine the top five businesses in your industry. As I mentioned earlier, your valuable resource called the public library can help you with this task. And they will do so with great pleasure! Don't underestimate the importance of knowing what the potential competition is doing, and what lessons they've learned along the way.

4. Examine what your competition is doing right. Discover how the top five companies in your field of interest are communicating with and selling to your database. You can do this by calling the top five and pretending to be a customer. Ask them to send you their sales literature. Solicit their mailing pieces. Visit with their top sales people. Let their telemarketers try to sell you. What benefits do they emphasize and what features do they brag about? Your business can benefit from all the information that you gather, and this is a great way to learn from the mistakes that other companies have already made.

Part of thoroughly researching a company is contacting the CEO. A friend of mine did this when she and her brother started a bakery. They studied all the information they could find on the competition, focusing especially on Mrs. Field's Cookies. Then her brother called the corporate office and spoke directly to Debbie Fields. She was impressed that he had done his homework on her company and was very helpful. She asked that he keep her posted on his progress. Most CEOs are more approachable than you might think. They're interested in new businesses because they're generally people oriented. If they are smart, they will take your call, or at least lead you to a Vice President who can give you the information you need.

When you contact the CEO, tell them that you are just starting a business in the same field, and that you admire such and such about their company (this will let them know that you have indeed done your homework). Ask if they would mind answering a few questions. Ask them, "What would you do differently if you were starting your business over again?" and "What are some of the major lessons that you've learned so far?" Then listen carefully to their responses. Take notes! Toward the end of your conversation, if they have not answered this question yet, your final question should be, "What advice would you give to a newcomer in this industry?" Again, listen carefully and ask any questions that come to mind. Never be afraid to ask questions. If they feel pressed for time, they will say so.

Always end your conversation by thanking them for their time and advice. Send a thank-you letter to express your appreciation and to establish a relationship for the future.

5. Identify the service, feature or information that is missing from the top five competitors. If you were going to buy their service, product or information, what improvements would you make? Get very analytical. Tear it apart. Remember you are looking for your niche—something that is easy to use and provides quick results.

6. *Create a competitive edge.* This is done by position-ing your product in the market place better than anyone else. Remember, if people have to choose between easy and hard, they will choose easy every time. If they have to choose between fast and slow, they will choose fast every time. If they must choose between simple and complicated, they will take simple every time. In order to gain a competitive edge your product or service must be faster, smaller, simpler, easier, more efficient, more secure, prettier, more featured, more valued, better advertised, more available and cost less than anything else out there in your field of expertise.

7. *Create a dynamite ad.* Marketing is the key that could make you a fortune. You must create advertising that catches the eye and causes the reader or viewer to *act.* Get books from the library or local bookstore and study this subject. Here are some tips for your adver-tisement:

* The headline should state precisely the ultimate benefit and competitive advantage of your product or service.
* Your ad copy should emphasize in exact detail the ultimate benefit of your product to the consumer.
* The copy should emphasize as many benefits as your space will allow.

Of secondary importance are the features of the product or service. Features describe the product or service. Benefits are what your customers receive when they use it. When you talk about your product, you are present-ing features. When you talk about results, you are presenting benefits. Your customers care more about benefits (what they will get out of it) than features. Spend more time and ad space on *results.*

Emotions outsell logic every time. Most businesses emphasize benefits because they create more emotion in the customer than features. Features appeal to the customer's logic and are important, but benefits outsell features because they appeal to the customer's emotions. Logic is an important part of a sale, but only after the emotions are engaged.

8. Run a limited test on your target database. Mail out a sample of your advertisement to your mailing list. Get feedback via the telephone using a very short survey, or see how many orders you receive. If you don't get enough orders, ask a few specific questions about your ad when you take your survey. Then run regular newspaper classified ads to see what response you get.

9. Keep testing your database with various ads until you have a 1% response rate. Rework your ads and keep testing until you find a message that pulls in a minimum of 1% response.

10. Test different media. Test as many different media as possible to see which are most cost effective and will generate the greatest amount of sales.

11. Undertake a major marketing campaign. If you want major results, you must do major marketing using a combination of different media and strategies, such as newspaper and television ads, flyers, brochures, and taking the time to meet people face-to-face. Run four or five marketing strategies concurrently with each other and keep them going, rotating new ones in periodically.

12. Market other versions of your product or service. Once you have a winning ad for a winning product, and you have rolled out a dynamite marketing campaign, start researching your next product. There are many businesses out there and all of them started with one idea. You may have had ideas in the past but did not act upon them. No matter how great the idea is, you must take an action step to make it happen in your life. Too many people sit and dream about being in business for themselves, and never take the first step. Fear is the main reason. They are afraid that they will fail and possibly lose a great deal of money. By learning as much as you can about business and studying the ideas in this book, you will greatly reduce your risk. You will approach business with an *educated* risk. It is better to try and fail than to never try at all. The only way you can fail is to never try! You were made to create, so don't hold yourself back!

From a very young age my children heard me say, "I would rather be poor and be in business for myself, than be rich and be in business for someone else." At least when you are in business for yourself you have the potential to create whatever level of success you choose. When you work for someone else, they choose your level of success for you.

I challenge you to take the first step in going into business for yourself— *decide that you will do it.* The next step is to act on that decision. Although it sounds simple, many people will work their entire life for a gold watch and a few dollars a month retirement from their employers. Why is it that more people are not willing to take that first step? It's because they find it easier to let someone else control their lives.

Why not make a decision today to experience the true American dream of being in business for yourself? Decide that you are willing to do whatever it takes to make your business a success. Perform the necessary preparation mentioned in this book. Put in the necessary time. Do what ever it takes to be in business for yourself.

Don't say you'll *try* going into business for yourself. Trying is never good enough. Make the decision. Decide to do it, or not. The same is true with any decision in your life. Make the decision. Make a plan. Stick to it.

Chapter 22 Review
Cashing In On Your Ideas

By using this twelve-step action plan, you can cash in on those great ideas in your head.

1. Identify or create a mailing list (database).

2. Do market research.

3 Determine the top five businesses in your chosen industry.

4. Evaluate what your competition is doing right.

5. Identify what services, features or information is missing from the top five competitors.

6. Create a competitive edge.

7. Create a dynamic ad that focuses on results and benefits, and elicits powerful positive emotions.

8. Using your ad, run a limited test on your target data base.

9. Keep testing your data base with various ads until you have a 1% response rate.

10. Test different media.

11. Undertake a major marketing campaign.

12. Market other versions of your product or service.

CHAPTER 23

UPGRADE

THE ONLY ONES AMONG
YOU WHO WILL REALLY BE
HAPPY ARE THOSE WHO WILL
HAVE SOUGHT AND FOUND
HOW TO SERVE.

ALBERT SCHWEITZER

*

IT IS NOT GOD'S WILL MERELY
THAT WE SHOULD BE HAPPY,
BUT THAT WE SHOULD MAKE
OURSELVES HAPPY.

IMMANUEL KANT

*

THE JOURNEY TO HAPPINESS
INVOLVES FINDING THE COURAGE
TO GO DOWN INTO OURSELVES
AND TAKE RESPONSIBILITY FOR
WHAT'S THERE: ALL OF IT.

RICHARD ROHR

My friend, Tom, taught me a powerful word—upgrade. This means to be better than you were the day before. This doesn't just deal with your finances, but every aspect of your life. If you are in a relationship, make an effort to upgrade that relationship every day. The same goes for your job, your life, and of course, your money. When you make an earnest effort to upgrade daily, you can't help but become successful.

My life is centered around serving others. My purpose in writing this book is to make this world a better place for more of us. If this information has helped to change some of your thoughts and concepts around money, share it with others. We are all in this life together and have an inherited obligation to serve each other. I envision seeing this book in everyone's library! May prosperity be yours all the days of your life.

The best tombstone I ever saw read, "While he was alive, he *lived!*" Remember to keep in mind what we are all supposed to be doing here—we are here to experience happiness. When you're making a decision about anything, first ask yourself, "Will this bring me happiness?" Then ask, "*How* will this bring me happiness?" Of course, you must be sensitive to the needs of those around you. Don't be destructive to others (or yourself) in your pursuit of happiness. However, by asking these questions before proceeding with any decision, you will be able to avoid needless journeys. These needless and wasted experiences are the ones which would not bring you happiness. Since we are all seeking the magical state of happiness, why don't we evaluate things from that perspective first? After all, it's your decision! T.S. Elliot said, "If you haven't the strength to impose your own terms upon life, you must accept the terms it offers you."

Don't let this book become a dust collector on your shelf. My intention is to create a thirst in you for more information on creating substantial wealth as well as a balanced, rich inner life.

A Native American Story

The Creator gathered all of Creation together and said, "I want to hide something from the humans until they are ready for it. It is the realization that they create their own reality."

The eagle said, "Give it to me, I will take it to the moon."

The Creator said, "No. One day they will go there and find it."

The salmon said, "Give it to me, I will bury it on the bottom of the ocean."

The Creator said, "No. They will go there too."

The buffalo said, "Give it to me, I will bury it on the Great Plains."

The Creator said, "No. They will cut into the skin of Mother Earth and find it even there."

Grandmother Mole, who lives in the breast of Mother Earth and who sees only with spiritual eyes, said, "Put it inside of them. It is the last place they will look."

The Creator said, "It is done."

Are you ready to *discover* and *use* the power inside you to create your own reality? Everyone is looking for the secret, when the secret is inside you all along. Realize that life is meant to be lived with *passion!* Seize each day and get the most out of it by putting yourself wholly into it. It is when we put value on our lives that our lives become valuable. Why not accept this truth: You have the power within to change whatever it is you do not like about your life.

If you have lack in any area, discover where it is and make a decision to change it. Make a plan to materialize it, and take an action step daily to experience it. Soon the lack will turn to prosperity, and you will know you have become truly empowered and successful beyond your wildest dreams.

Why not return to the beginning of this book with the attitude of finding your pot of gold? And knowing that you can! Start from the beginning and reread every word as if your life depended on it. Take notes so you can reinforce your learning. If you miss even one important point in this book, it could be the exact point you needed to *ignite the fire* in your life!

Chapter 23 Review
Upgrade

1. When you make an earnest effort to upgrade daily, you cannot help but become successful.

2. When you make a decision about anything, first ask yourself, "Will this bring me happiness"? Then ask, "*How* will this bring me happiness"?

3. Realize that life was meant to be lived. Seize each day and get the most out of it. When we put value on our lives, our lives become valuable.

4. Accept the fact that you have the power to change whatever you do not like about your life. If you are lacking in any area, find it and make a decision to change it. Act on it. And stick with it.

5. Return to the beginning of this book with the attitude of finding *your* pot of gold. Reread every word as if your life depended on it. Take notes to reinforce your learning. If you miss even one important point it could be the exact point you need to ignite your life's passion.

Conclusion

As we part, my friend, I trust you to truly realize the power you were born with—the power to create! God is the most powerful force in the universe, whose nature and essence is creative. This power is inside you! You were born with it. It is your birthright. And you access it through the power of decision.

Don't waste this incredible power by settling for a mediocre life! Do your very best to learn the information in this book, use it, and then teach others what you have learned and experienced. When you share the knowledge you have gained to help others become prosperous and fulfill their dreams, then you are truly wealthy!

I bid you, and the generations that follow you, wealth overflowing! Because you are willing to put forth the necessary effort to upgrade your life, you will make a positive difference in the world around you. When you accomplish this, you set others free to do the same!

Many blessings!

For additional copies of

Breaking The Money Barriers

call ACCESS Publishers Network

1-800-345-0096

Now order these additional items as gifts or to complete your own financial library !

Breaking The Money Barriers Workbook	$15.95
Breaking The Money Barriers Book	$19.95
Breaking The Money Barriers Book on Audio Tape	$29.95
Simple Stock Market Book	$19.95
Simple Stock Market Book on Audio Tape	$59.95

Add $3.00 **per book** USA shipping and handling, or $4.00 per book international shipping and handling. UPS 2ND DAY delivery add $10.00 USA only.

Credit Card Orders: Visa & Master Card only

☐☐☐☐☐☐☐☐☐☐☐☐☐☐☐☐☐☐☐ Exp. date ☐☐☐☐
                                        (mo) (yr)

Full name on card:_____

PLEASE PRINT CLEARLY

Signature:_____

Title	Price	No.	Total

Autograph to: *(print clearly)*	**Subtotal**	
	Shipping	
	Total Enclosed	

Ship To:

Name_____

Address_____

City _____ State _____ Zip _____

Country _____ Telephone _____

Enclose check or money order payable to Michael Duckett. Mail to: Dynamic Consulting, P.O. Box 669426, Marietta, GA 30066-0108

Are you fed up with *wishing* for more money in your life?

Then this book is for you! Dr. Duckett has created a technology based on researching more than 1,000 self-made millionaires. These simple step-by-step techniques have helped over 9,000 people become millionaires in an extraordinarily short period of time.

You'll learn -
- Simple steps to attract money to you like a magnet
- The twelve beliefs all wealthy people teach their children
- The energy of money and the basic truths all millionaires use in their lives
- How the concept of exchange keeps money flowing easily into your life
- A simple time management tool that will change your life forever
- How to conquer fear once and for all
- How to develop mental self-discipline
- A simple ancient exercise to discover your life-purpose and how to make money with it
- The wealth accumulation secret of King Solomon that works today
- Seven wealth principles all prosperous people share
- How to develop true internal power and use it to bring money into your life
- How to set up a part-time home business for increased income
- How to upgrade your life daily
- How to make your dreams come true by breaking all of the money barriers
- And much, much more!

Dr. Mike Duckett started from an impoverished background and is a self-made multi-millionaire whose mission is to teach others how to become financially independent through knowledge, inner strength and balance in life. Mike is a life-long student holding degrees in Business, Psychology, Law, Biology, Chemistry, Chiropractic, Nutrition and Theology.

$19.95 US   **Finance**

ISBN 0-9668107-0-8

51995

9 780966 810707